Designing History

Designing History

The Extraordinary Art & Style of the Obama White House

Michael S. Smith

with Margaret Russell

Foreword by Michelle Obama

RIZZOLI
NEW YORK

New York Paris London Milan

CONTENTS

FOREWORD

Growing up, home was the second floor of a tidy brick bungalow on Euclid Avenue in the South Shore neighborhood of Chicago. It was nightly dinners with my mother, my father, and my brother. It was the sound of John Coltrane or Ella Fitzgerald from my dad's record player, the sight of a tray of toothpicked pigs in a blanket on New Year's Eve. It was lunch hours spent playing jacks with my friends, birthdays with all my cousins crowded around the kitchen table, cracking jokes.

Home was a specific place, with specific people and specific memories. But more than that, it was a specific *feeling.* It was comfort and warmth and security, an enveloping richness of our family's story — a place where my brother and I could speak our minds, make mistakes, and begin the lifelong process of becoming. It was ours, and ours alone.

Years later, when I became a mother myself, I wanted nothing more than to re-create that sense of comfort and stability for my own children. My husband and I had done our best to achieve it in our home in Chicago, but when the vortex of a presidential campaign concluded and sent our family to the White House, my biggest worry was the most basic: Would our daughters be able to have a childhood that in any way approached normalcy?

The White House is where President Roosevelt forged battle plans with his admirals and generals to defeat the Axis in World War II. It's where President Lincoln signed the Emancipation Proclamation. It's an office where policies are enacted, where deals are made. It's a museum where visitors — sometimes hundreds, sometimes thousands — pass through almost every day.

And it's a place where real families with real lives spend four or eight years together, in and out of the spotlight. So in addition to its vital role in our democracy, I also needed the space

OPPOSITE: First Lady Michelle Obama on the front porch of her family's Georgian Revival home in the Hyde Park neighborhood of Chicago as she was about to kick off the international book tour for her groundbreaking memoir, *Becoming.*

to play a very practical purpose—a place where our girls could sprawl out on the floor with their Polly Pockets and stuffed animals, where they could invite friends over for popcorn and a movie, where they could play ball in the halls and go outside to play in the snow.

Living in the White House with a young family, I know now, is something like conducting a symphony. Creating a space that can fulfill the public demands of my husband's role as Head of State and Commander in Chief and ours as First Family, a space that can shoulder the weight of history, and a space that welcomes the daily rhythms of a family—it's all placed on the same musical staff, the notes playing off one another. Achieving a harmony, with the right rhythm and melodies, is something that can only be achieved with practice.

Thankfully, we had help. I first met Michael Smith shortly after my husband was elected, in the mad swirl of the transition. Immediately, he understood that we were a young family with two little girls who preferred Crate & Barrel over antique credenzas and a grandmother who bristled a bit at any whiff of pomp. But we were also the Obamas: the first Black residents of the White House. The pressure on any First Family is enormous. The pressure on the first Black one would be even greater. Michael never lost sight of that. He made sure our values and vision for America—one based in inclusivity and a love for all of its people—were reflected in every detail of this remarkable home.

You can see his touch in the artwork he helped us choose to display on the walls, American innovators like Alma Thomas, Edward Ruscha, and Robert Rauschenberg. You can see it in the furniture he selected, which showcased the craftsmanship of everyday American woodworkers, and in the Old Family Dining Room on the State Floor, a public room we designed with modern decor and opened up to tourists for the first time in history. And you can see it in the thoughtful upgrades to the private residence's lighting, a massive project that Michael undertook with respect and care. It probably will surprise no one to learn the White House, with all its immaculate grandeur, tends to do things old-school. When we arrived, most rooms still relied on the twinkle of crystal chandeliers as a primary light source. These chandeliers are gorgeous works of art unto themselves, but they weren't always the most practical choices for bringing warm light into a family space or illuminating the masterpieces hanging in our halls.

So Michael brought in the tools of modernity. A little recessed lighting here, a dimmer there. And, like that, the Monet painting hanging outside my bedroom door and the Degas sculpture in our dining room became newly vibrant, newly alive. Good friends would walk by a piece and ask, "Has that always been there?" And we'd say, "Well, yes, you just couldn't see it before." That's the magic of Michael—shining a light on the past to bring more life to the present. With meticulous research, he paid homage to our history while also understanding that any choice we made was making history as well. Because in this space, everything—from the words uttered in passing to the napkins used at dinner—becomes history in a few years or a few decades.

Finally, and perhaps most importantly, from his very first projects, Michael helped us foster the warmth and comfort for our family that I'd hoped. Our daughters had rooms to call their own, where they could swap out a great work of art for a poster or a photo of their friends. There were cozy couches to cuddle up with our dogs, Bo and Sunny, after a long day. And I had my own space where I could hide out in sweatpants and catch up on bad TV. The residence became a true refuge where our family could simply be a family, where our girls could grow into young women with voices of their own.

For eight years at the White House, we lived and loved, made mistakes and made progress. We're so grateful for the help of not only Michael, but also all of the ushers, butlers, house-keepers, curators, chefs, florists, gardeners, engineers, volunteers, and so many others who embraced our family and helped make the White House our home—while always upholding its magnificent history and unparalleled traditions.

And while my mom's trays of pigs in a blanket were sometimes replaced by tuxedoed professionals passing canapés, we celebrated many holidays together. Some of my warmest memories were decorating the Christmas tree with our girls, *A Charlie Brown Christmas* softly playing in the background. Those same cousins who crowded around our kitchen table during childhood came to the White House each Thanksgiving, crowding around a television in the East Room, with priceless portraits of George and Martha Washington keeping us company there, too.

And on most nights, around the dinner table, the rhythm of our family churned forward—mom, dad, and two siblings, sharing stories about our days, cracking jokes, and strengthening the bonds that define our family. We may have been a long way from a little bungalow on Euclid Avenue, but we weren't far from home at all. What I know now is that home isn't somewhere you go—it's something you create.

—Michelle Obama, November 2019

PREFACE

Every time you walk into the White House, you can't help but feel the intense power of more than two centuries of storied American history; the very experience of being in those fabled rooms is exhilarating. But while the building itself is important — its silhouette firmly etched into the American psyche — the White House is essentially static without the soul and spirit of the people within. It's their character, intellect, and humanity that make it so compelling.

My work with the White House was deeply personal. I was always very conscious that the Obamas were a dynamic but actually super normal young family that had been placed in extraordinary circumstances. I had to balance the logistics of creating a comfortable home for them within the context of not only this historic house, but their historic presidency, where every decision, large or small, was driven by their uncommon mindfulness. The Obamas were my constant inspiration, and their mission to celebrate the White House as the People's House, a place that was welcoming and accessible to all Americans, led to our focus on highlighting the best of America in every possible way — through not just the diversity of creative talents, but the diversity and richness of culture — from painting and sculpture to the craft of furniture, textiles, ceramics, and more.

This book documents the various projects we worked on together, the fascinating interiors and first families from the past that informed our decisions, and the art and style of the rooms we created for this family. This is a family that not only respected the tradition and the weight of the history of the house that was their home, but also appreciated the profound need to bring it into the modern age. For me, having a small role in this remarkable evolution will remain one of the greatest honors of my life.

—Michael S. Smith, May 2020

OPPOSITE: As one who loves history, there are a number of White House rooms that I am captivated with for so many different reasons, but my favorite will always be the Yellow Oval Room, which was essentially the Obama family's living room. I wanted to re-create for them some of the glamour that was instilled there by President and Mrs. Kennedy in the 1960s.

1 THE DECORATOR–ELECT

The way in which I originally connected with Michelle and Barack Obama was unbelievably indirect, so much so that it never seemed possible that I would end up working in the White House. Like many of life's most meaningful relationships, it was serendipitous, almost accidental. There were so many moving parts, and at times it seemed like it would never come to fruition. And yet this became the most extraordinary adventure and, ultimately, one of the greatest honors and joys of my life.

It all started with Katherine Chez Malkin, a dear friend who lives in Chicago and is married to the real estate developer Judd Malkin. We'd met several years earlier when she hired me for a new project that her husband's firm was building in California. Our business collaboration led to a close friendship, and I ended up working on both their house in Palm Springs and their very beautiful Art Deco duplex in Chicago. After Barack Obama won the 2008 presidential election, Katherine and I had been on the phone, musing over what the White House redecoration should be. We bounced ideas in a completely blue-sky way about different artists and artisans, the creative voices who might be part of the new Obama culture, and what we hoped the DNA of this young family moving into the traditionally staid White House might be.

Crazily, Desirée Rogers—a prominent Chicago businesswoman and the former wife of John Rogers, a longtime Obama friend and supporter—who had just been announced as the new social secretary to the White House, was friendly with the Malkins and happened to live in the same apartment building. Though the whole design world was abuzz at the time with rumors about the front-runners to become the Obamas' decorator, with many well-known names tossed about, it never really occurred to me that I would be one of them. But after we had a few more conversations about the project, Katherine called me and firmly declared, "I'm going to get you this job." When I laughed, she responded that

OPPOSITE: The Obama family on the night of November 4, 2008, about to take the stage in Grant Park, Chicago, where the president-elect would deliver his historic victory speech to an enthusiastic crowd estimated at more than 240,000 people.

she was quite serious—reminding me that she knew Desirée—and asked how fast I could send her copies of my design books, including *Houses*, which had just been released. She planned to enclose a note and leave them for Desirée with their doorman. After much running around (both books had apparently sold out in Chicago, which was great, though not helpful, news), we tracked them down in a Lake Forest bookshop, had the books delivered to Katherine, and sent this complete pipe dream off on its merry way.

For as long as I can remember, I've been a supporter of liberal and progressive causes,

and my partner, James Costos, and I have always been Democrats. We knew and greatly admired Hillary Clinton from when she was first lady, and then a senator of New York, and though I hadn't ever met Barack Obama, he deeply impressed me from the outset. Once he gained the party's nomination, we enthusiastically supported him, and the more I saw of him and his wonderful young family on the campaign trail, the more hopeful I became. They were incredibly inspiring—smart, natural, and completely lacking in pretension.

FROM TOP: The Chicago penthouse I designed for my friends Katherine and Judd Malkin, who happened to live in the same building as Desirée Rogers. My books, *Elements of Style* and *Houses*, which Katherine hand-delivered to Desirée. OPPOSITE: The recommendation letter Katherine generously wrote on my behalf.

KATHERINE MALKIN

Dear Desiree,

I hope that you view my interest in this as "passionate" and not "wacky." I truly mean to be helpful.

Here are five reasons that I feel Michael Smith is the perfect fit for the Obama family:

1. He is a genius—by every definition of the word. He perfectly fits what has been the apparent mantra of the incoming administration.
   a. He is the top in his field.
   b. He mobilizes and moves at the speed of lightning.
   c. He has an appreciation of the historical with a fresh approach.
   d. He stands by his convictions.
   e. He is socially responsible.
2. He understands that a family's comfort is paramount to the design process.
3. He will find a way to be fiscally and morally responsible, and still deliver a product that will make both the Obama family and our country, comfortable and proud.
4. He understands and protects the privacy of his clients.
5. He will make you laugh.

I believe in my heart of hearts that Michael Smith will become known as the best interiors person of our century—bar none.

Once again, I am so thrilled for you. You have an enormous job ahead of you and there could be no one more capable. I saw Karen this morning and we are hoping to be able to toast this occasion before you leave.

Have the happiest of Thanksgivings and say hello to Victoria for me.

Fondly,

Katherine

At the time, James was an executive at HBO, and while we both traveled constantly for business, we wanted to be home in Los Angeles on this historic Election Day to cast our votes in person. We watched the returns that evening with a big group of people at the house of a close friend, and I remember how excited and thrilled we all were when it became clear that Obama had a winning lead over Senator John McCain. But I also remember thinking that night how overwhelming it must have been for his young family to walk out on that stage in Chicago; the girls seemed so small and vulnerable surrounded by that jubilant, celebratory crowd that numbered more than 240,000. Then I saw the energy and strength of Michelle Obama as she stepped forward to speak, wearing that striking Narciso Rodriguez dress—she looked radiant, poised, and fearless. I felt that all was well with the nation in that moment.

The Obamas were a couple we could identify with, people we could understand. For any of us who felt like we were "others"—whether we were gay, Jewish, female, African American, Latino, or anyone who had ever felt marginalized or disenfranchised—this was a new, fresh moment for America. It was very, very uplifting. And considering the financial meltdown the country was facing, Obama's election signaled the possibility that progress would be made in a balanced way, very much for the protection and advancement of the many, not just the few.

It was late when we headed home after the Chicago acceptance-speech coverage. I remember getting into my car on that quiet, dark street, turning to James, and—without uttering a word—literally bursting into tears from the combined stress and extraordinary joy of the day.

Around three weeks after the election, we were in Jamaica for Thanksgiving. Out of the blue,

OPPOSITE, FROM TOP: Barack Obama in his Chicago living room. The Obamas' spacious Georgian Revival house, located in the city's Hyde Park neighborhood; they left it basically intact when they moved to the White House. ABOVE: The Obama family at home in Chicago, before the 2008 presidential campaign had begun.

I got a phone call from Desirée Rogers saying that the Obamas would be very interested in talking to me about the White House project. It was surreal. Though it felt like it must be a joke, I realized it really was Desirée, and she wasn't being funny—and despite the fact that I was sitting on a secluded stretch of sandy beach on vacation, I had to take what was happening with the utmost seriousness. Through a series of calls over the weekend, Desirée provided more details on what needed to be done, as well as how fast, and I was able to put together an idea of the scope of the project and draft an extremely rough budget. Then, on our last day, just as we were leaving the island, Desirée phoned once more to tell me that the Obamas had, in fact, chosen me to be their White House decorator. I was overwhelmed and deeply honored, though having worked with so many clients over the years, I knew that this would not be definite until we could sit down together to talk and make sure that we shared a strong connection.

I did my best to keep my excitement in check—which was helped by the fact that I was sworn to secrecy. Only James and my closest assistants were aware that I flew to Chicago to visit the Obamas the first week of December, just after Thanksgiving. In advance of my meeting, Desirée and I discussed the logistics of the project for several hours at her apartment. Then a car took us to see my potential new clients at their house, which is not far from the University of Chicago. It was a late fall afternoon and getting dark as our car approached their street, which was blocked off on both sides by the Secret Service. When

we asked the driver to let us out nearby, he turned in his seat and said, very proudly, "You know, the Obamas live near here." Silently rolling our eyes in amusement at each other, Desirée and I replied, practically in unison, "Wow, that's amazing."

As we walked up the blockaded street, I spotted their home, a brick Georgian Revival with white trim, set back from the street and with a generous porch in front. Once inside, I saw that it had a sophisticated, academic appeal. I grew up in California, and the house immediately reminded me of the kind one might find in Pasadena—the ground floor was spacious and airy, with beamed ceilings, gleaming wood

ABOVE: I didn't create an elaborate presentation for my initial meeting with Michelle Obama. She made it clear that the rooms for her daughters, Malia and Sasha, were her top priority, so I brought her some tear sheets, a range of paint chips, and colorful fabric and wallpaper swatches in bold patterns.

floors, and dramatic Arts and Crafts–style millwork. Elegant and inviting, it looked like a perfect family home. The living room was an intelligent fusion of the Midwest and exotic, far-off places, with tailored sofas and chairs and chest-high bookshelves filled with wonderful books and curious objects the Obamas had gathered on their travels. There was a striking red Chinese table in the dining room, and the president-elect's Grammy, won for his audiobook recording of *Dreams from My Father*, was casually perched on a shelf in the library. The house glowed with the warmth of wood and was thoughtful, layered, and cozy. Honestly, if you were a set decorator, it's exactly the place you would have created for that family to live in.

Michelle Obama walked in not a moment later, gracious and welcoming, greeting me with a big smile. The three of us sat at the dining table and ended up talking for a few hours about design ideas and how the family lived. Prompted by Desirée telling me that Mrs. Obama had mentioned that she wanted "pops of color" for the girls, I brought her a small presentation of some fabric and wallpaper samples, paint swatches, and suggestions for Malia's and Sasha's rooms. It had been decades since children that young had lived in the White House—when Jimmy Carter was elected president in 1976, Amy Carter was nine years old, and Sasha was about to be the youngest child to move in since John F. Kennedy, Jr. arrived, barely eight weeks old, in January 1961. I wanted their bedrooms to incorporate classic American iconography in a colorful way, one that was cheerful and fun, mindful both of the historic import and prominence of the White House and the fact that Sasha and Malia were only seven and ten years old.

The overriding message from that initial meeting was how important the Obamas' children are to them and that they would be the top priority. "We have to make the White House comfortable for our daughters," was Mrs. Obama's primary directive, one that she would repeat often in the weeks ahead. The move was going to be an enormous disruption for the girls, taking them out of school and away from their friends. Mrs. Obama's main concern was not for her husband or herself, but that this huge change in their daughters' lives should be softened in every way possible. As each would have her own bedroom and bath, I would need to create two cheerful, private spaces where they could be themselves and hang out with their new friends, completely protected from public scrutiny.

I was briefly introduced to Sasha and Malia and ended up showing Malia my ideas for her room; I was relieved when she seemed enthusiastic about the bright colors and patterns. Then Mrs. Obama took us on an extensive tour of their home, including a newly redone family TV room and the bedrooms they had decorated for the girls. I got the sense from walking through the house with her that she and her husband would likely want to invest more in their chil-

dren's rooms at the White House, rather than their own. It was essential that Sasha and Malia would feel as comfortable living in Washington as they did at their home in Chicago.

We headed back downstairs, and suddenly Barack Obama strode in, extending a very firm handshake. "Please call me Barack," he said, though this was the first and last time I did for nearly the next decade. (As I would learn, the appropriate form of address would remain an issue. It was hard to be formal with such a young, friendly couple, but at the same time everyone needed to show appropriate respect. It didn't seem correct to use first names, yet calling them Mr. President or Mrs. Obama sometimes sounded too stiff and formal. In the months ahead, the White House staff and I would usually go into verbal contortions to avoid using any names or titles at all, and we often resorted to the traditional, ever-useful acronyms POTUS and FLOTUS.) "You have a very cool demeanor," the president-elect told me. "I suspect you must be really good at this." I liked that he was so direct—and that he seemed to believe in me—and I was immediately reassured about working with him, though still not absolutely convinced that I would be.

OPPOSITE: The excitement about Barack Obama's victory extended from Harlem to Hollywood. ABOVE: A now iconic image of Michelle and Barack Obama and their young daughters, Sasha (*left*) and Malia, in Grant Park, prior to the president-elect's acceptance speech. I was filled with emotion that night, hopeful about this new, fresh moment for America.

As I was leaving, Mrs. Obama gave me a warm hug, and the president-elect turned to me and said, "Just think, when they write a book about my administration, you'll be in it." Hearing Barack Obama say this was an almost out-of-body experience. "Let's see how it goes" was all I managed to muster in response.

Obama was joking, of course, but he had already zoomed ahead, thinking far into the future — which made the importance of the role I was about to take on even more apparent and more intimidating. The juxtaposition of being with this lovely family in their warm, personal home on a normal Midwestern street while contemplating working for them in the White House made it clear that something extraordinary was about to happen. And the Obamas were certainly aware of this seismic shift and beginning to understand its repercussions. It's been said that no candidate or their family ever believes they are going to win up until the last moment, and I suspect that was the case with Michelle and Barack Obama. In less than two months, they would be moving from a charming house that meant so much to their family to "the People's House" — an imposing 55,000-square-foot, 132-room structure that was managed by a staff of nearly 100. How could any of us imagine all that would entail and the profound changes that their lives would undergo?

I have always been obsessed with history, and I realized that I was about to be closely involved with two people — who were at that moment arguably the most famous people in the world — during a truly remarkable time of transformation for our nation. Throughout my career, which started in my early 20s, I have been incredibly lucky to work for all sorts of highly successful clients from a wide range of fields — fashion, film, real estate, finance, etc. — but I knew that this would be different. It would be different in scale, complexity, and the level of scrutiny. I had never dealt with this degree of public adulation; or the sheer euphoria and joy that surrounded Barack Obama's win, the energy and excitement that greeted his every action; or the weight of the expectations that surrounded him and his family every day.

I was acutely aware that the work that my firm would do for the Obamas must always be beyond reproach. One of my responsibilities would be to protect the privacy of the president-elect and his family, but I knew I must also be meticulous in preventing any potential breach of ethics regarding anything we might purchase on their behalf or allowing anyone to wrongly benefit from an association with them. Throughout their lives, Barack and Michelle Obama had worked to reflect the highest standards of American character and integrity, and I wasn't ever going to be the one to prompt a misstep.

It was then that the real meaning of that moment began to dawn on me, and I was filled with an adrenaline rush of how to get started. My role would be to work with the Obamas to establish a presidential residence in one of the world's most iconic buildings, a house with a storied history but a strangely fluid identity, one that has adapted to the aesthetics and lifestyle of each successive president and his family. I would have to craft a foundation for the Obamas' private lives within a grand and overwhelming building full of ceremony, security, and staff. It had to be accomplished without fanfare or drama, on a modest budget, and within the constraints of the vast numbers of rules, regulations, and traditions that accompany such an official undertaking. To me, the top priority was to create as much impact in the Residence as quickly as possible — starting well before they moved in — so that after the inauguration, they could immediately feel comfortable and at ease in their new home. I hardly understood what I was in for. But I knew I couldn't wait to begin.

ABOVE: A London newspaper vendor with the November 5, 2008, edition of *The Times*. Barack Obama's historic win dominated the global news media for weeks — and it was the beginning of a whole new world for me as well.

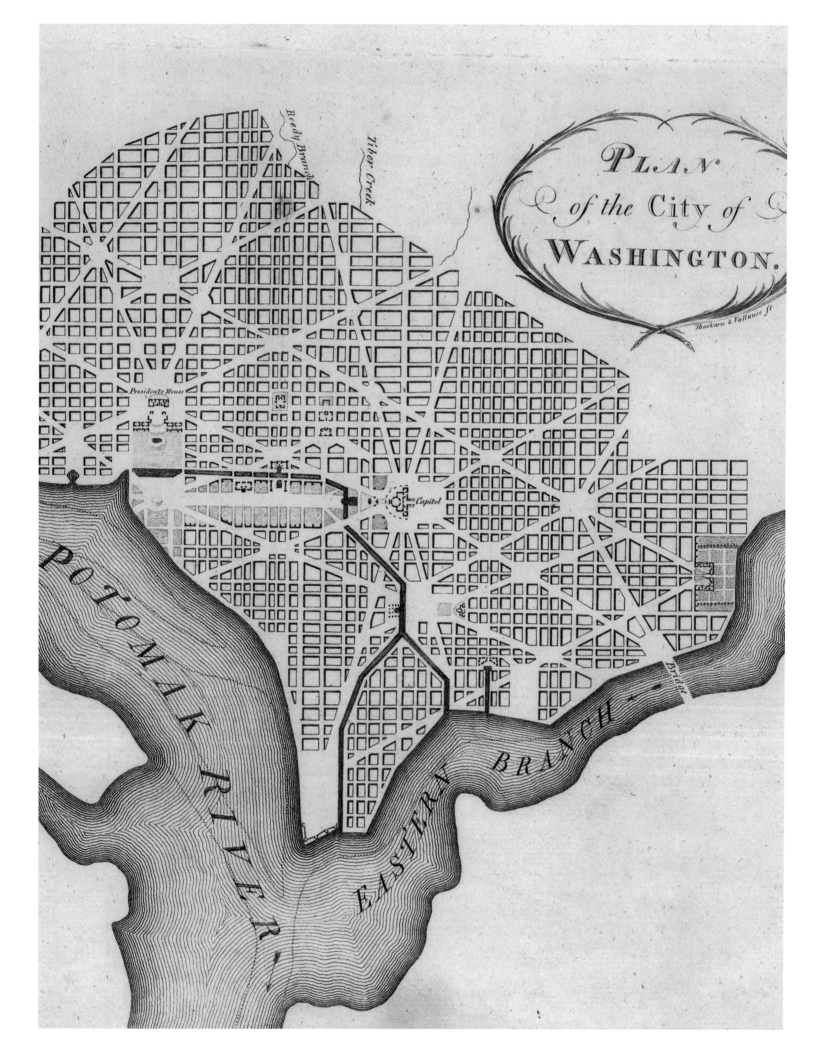

Reedy Branch

Tiber Creek

PLAN
of the City of
WASHINGTON.

Thackara & Vallance Sc

Presidents House

Capitol

POTOMAK RIVER

EASTERN BRANCH

Bridge

WHAT'S PAST IS PROLOGUE

Considering how iconic it is, and how deeply it resonates in the American imagination, the White House has been surprisingly controversial since it was conceived in the late 18th century—and it has undergone far more changes, expansions, modifications, and re-decorations than most of us realize. I've always been a student of history—especially the history of architecture and the decorative arts, which actually led to my being a designer—and I have a real love of American history as well. Once the Obamas asked me to work with them on this project, I became obsessed, immersing myself in the discovery of all one could know about this house, a building that was more than just famous, it was mythic. The White House is so multilayered—it was like examining the rings in a cross section of an ancient tree as I strove to understand the history of the building, as well as the intent and impact of each president and first family over the decades.

This was also a house with very specific conditions and requirements. There are rooms that are public, and rooms that are private. There are rooms with very, very tall ceilings, and rooms that are windowless and quite dark. There were structural and technical complications that I had to grapple with and try to improve as I worked to make the residence more livable and relevant for this vital, young family. I wanted my vision of the White House to incorporate the history of our nation and all of its diversity within the grandeur of its rooms but also be a warm, comfortable, and workable family home for at least the next four, if not eight, years. Above all, it needed to be appropriately personal for the Obamas, their two small children, and, ultimately, two rambunctious dogs.

I was dedicated to learning as much as I could about the house. To get a true sense of the

OPPOSITE: Major Pierre Charles L'Enfant's original, circa-1792 plan for the city of Washington, District of Columbia, which was founded in 1790. Elected president by a unanimous vote of the electoral college the previous year, George Washington had selected the location for the seat of the new federal government, as well as the sites for the U.S. Capitol and what was then called the President's House. President Washington hired L'Enfant, a French army engineer who fought in the American Revolution, to devise a plan for the new city, which placed the Capitol building, set high on a hill, at the center of a grid from which radiated wide boulevards.

past, I read as many original accounts as I could get my hands on, from first ladies' biographies and memoirs to Jacqueline Kennedy's letters, interviews with Betty Ford, Nancy Reagan, Hillary Clinton, and Laura Bush—even the biography of Kennedy decorator Sister Parish, long considered the doyenne of decoration. Not only were Mrs. Parish's interiors celebrated for their refined warmth, but her client list of old-guard American "aristocrats" also gave her extraordinary insight into what an elegant and appropriately youthful yet respectfully historic Kennedy White House should look like.

I was also incredibly lucky that five years earlier, in another crazy act of kismet through a dear friend, the late Casey Ribicoff, my longtime pal and the widow of Connecticut Senator Abraham Ribicoff, had thoughtfully seated me next to Mrs. Reagan at her son's wedding. Nancy Reagan and I ended up becoming phone friends, and when I took on this project I began to call her with questions about aspects of the house and what it was like to decorate the rooms when she was first lady—a time that many consider to be one of the warmest and most elegant renditions of the private spaces.

I had many interesting conversations with Mrs. Reagan, including once when I called her in L.A. from Paris and we spoke for a full four hours even though it was the middle of the night for me. I was pacing back and forth in my hotel room as I listened to her stories, riveted by the detailed information she shared; it was fascinating to see history through her eyes, as well as to learn about how she dealt with practical considerations. I remember discussing that I had read in her memoir how inordinately long it took to have curtains for the various upstairs rooms made, and I swore to her that I would make it a priority to have the Obamas' curtains finished in record time. (Window measurements for the second and third floors were among the first things I requested as we prepared for the move.) In truth, all the research was enormously satisfying and helpful. I wanted to be able to have the sense of almost picking the building up to study it from every angle to understand how it had arrived at this point. I was curious to know what had worked previously and what hadn't, and I was always thrilled by the constant thread of history that ran through all of the White House rooms. I was excited— though slightly in awe—by the prospect of becoming part of that history.

That history began in 1791, when President George Washington selected the site for the President's House in the District of Columbia, the new seat of government, and a competition for its design was announced. Irish-born architect James Hoban won the commission and its $500 prize with a structure said to be inspired by Leinster House, a mid-18th-century Georgian manor in Dublin that is now home to the Irish parliament. The next year, when

the design was revealed to the public and the house's cornerstone was laid, there was concern that perhaps it was too grand, too imperial, and that it might be inappropriate for the leader of a brand-new, democratic government in the Age of Enlightenment. Envisioned as something of a country villa, it was essentially an oversize version of what any member of the landed gentry might own. Built by laborers who were primarily African American—both enslaved and free—as well as local white artisans and workers and those who emigrated from Ireland, Scotland, and other European countries, at the time and for decades to come, it was considered to be the largest private residence in the United States.

Situated off the National Mall on the Washington city plan drawn up by French émigré, engineer, and architect Pierre Charles L'Enfant, the structure was set apart from the Capitol and other new government buildings, equal in importance but separate. Originally referred to as the Executive Mansion or the President's House, a distinction that is still evident in certain places (it's engraved on some presidential silver, for example, that is still in use), the building was set within an outsize park, an 82-acre garden that was reserved for the enjoyment of the president and his family but was also essentially public land—anyone could ride across the lawn or picnic there—an early indication of the very complicated dual role the White House has played throughout history. In layout, it was like a conventional country house, but the rooms were vast, the ceilings soared, and finishing the house and filling it with enough furnishings to make it feel even somewhat comfortable was daunting.

ABOVE: Leinster House, a mid-18th-century Georgian manor in Dublin that now serves as the home of the Irish parliament. It was said to be an inspiration for James Hoban, an Irish-born architect from Charleston, South Carolina, whose proposal won him the commission to design the official President's House in Washington in 1792.

After President Washington was elected in 1789, he and his wife, Martha, lived in Manhattan, the temporary seat of government, and then relocated to the official President's House in Philadelphia before construction of the White House began. John Adams, who took office in 1797 as the nation's second president, lived in the Philadelphia house with his wife, Abigail, and then moved into the White House in November 1800 though the eight-year project was far from complete. Gilbert Stuart's full-length portrait of George Washington, paid for by a Congressional allocation of $800, had been installed before their arrival and the furniture from their Philadelphia home was put in place, but there were still no steps leading to the front entrance, and so few rooms were usable that the first lady was forced to hang their laundry to dry in what is now the East Room.

Just one month later, in early December, President Adams lost the election to Thomas Jefferson, the vice president. The Adamses, who had been allotted a decoration allowance of $14,000, had lived in the mansion a mere four months, and it was still unfinished when President Jefferson, who had trained as an architect, took office and began to reimagine it to better suit his own aesthetic. Though he was a former U.S. minister to France and then President Washington's secretary of state, his enhancements to the house were not nec-

essarily inspired by the Continent. He made practical improvements, such as adding service wings and the East and West Colonnades and installing an early version of water closets on the top floor to replace outdoor privies. Jefferson opened the White House to the public in 1801 and five years later created an unusual museum in the Entrance Hall that focused on his fascination with Lewis and Clark's transformative expeditions to the western frontier. Until the end of his two terms in 1809, visitors were welcome to view the exhibition of antlers, animal pelts, crop specimens, and Native American headdresses and artifacts that he displayed in the grand space. James Madison was elected president in 1808 and won a second

OPPOSITE: An early-19th-century French soup tureen, one of 130 silver items purchased by President Andrew Jackson in 1833; it is engraved *President's House*, as is much of the White House silver still in use today. ABOVE: The President's House, on High Street in Philadelphia. President Washington and his wife, Martha, first lived in Manhattan after his inauguration, then moved to this house in Philadelphia, which was the temporary seat of government while Washington, D.C., was being established. After John Adams assumed office in 1797, he and his wife, Abigail, lived here before moving to Washington in 1800, as the White House neared completion.

The surrounding Ground was chiefly used for Brick yards,
it was enclosed in a rough post and rail fence — (1803)

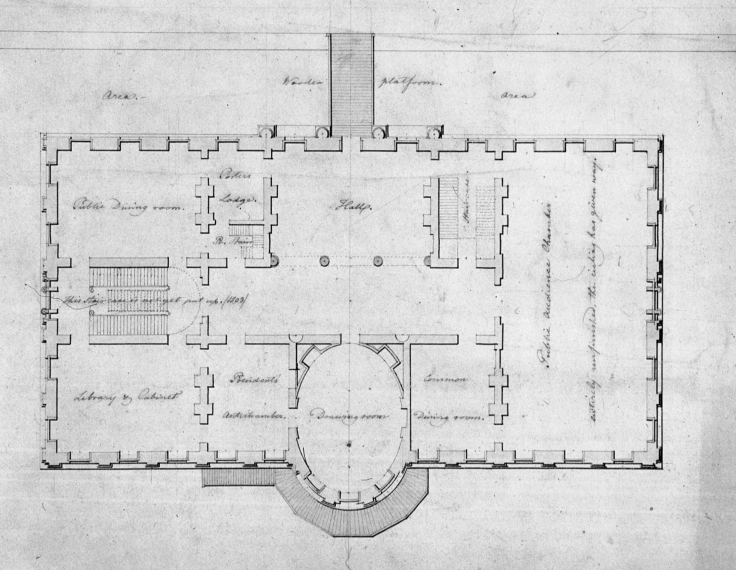

Wooden platform.

Area. —   area

Public Dining room.   Porters   Lodge.   Halls

                       P. Stair

This Stair case is not yet put up. (1803)

Library & Cabinet   President's   Common
                       Antichamber.   Drawing room   Dining room.

Public Audience Chamber
entirely unfinished, the ceiling has given way.

During the short residence of President Adams & Washington, the wooden Stairs & platform were the usual
entrance to the house, and the present drawing room was a mere Vestibule.

Plan of the Principal Story in 1803.

Henry Latrobe
1807.

OPPOSITE: An 1803 plan of the State Floor of President Thomas Jefferson's White House, drawn by Benjamin Henry Latrobe, the architect of the Capitol building, whom Jefferson had appointed Surveyor of the Public Buildings. ABOVE: An anonymous 1827 watercolor of the White House and its grounds. The South Portico had been add-

ed three years prior, during President James Monroe's administration; Jefferson's stone walls and President John Quincy Adams's tree nursery are also depicted. BELOW: An early-1800s architectural sketch of the north façade of the White House by Samuel Blodget, Jr.; the north façade is considered to be the principal entrance to the Residence.

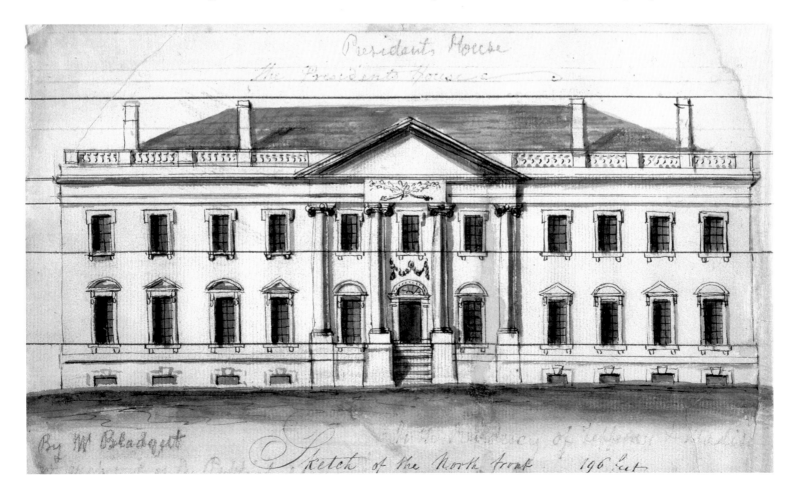

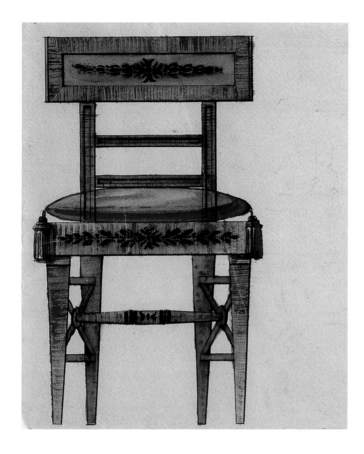

ABOVE: An 1809 drawing for a klismos-style chair by Benjamin Henry Latrobe, who designed a suite of furnishings for President James Madison and his wife, Dolley. RIGHT: Residue from the smoke and flames of the 1814 burning of the White House by British troops during the War of 1812. The charred stone was revealed in 1992, when nearly 30 layers of paint were stripped from the façade, part of a preservation project that took place from 1980 to 1996. BELOW: Based on a watercolor by George Munger, an aquatint engraving by William Strickland depicts a gutted White House after the fire. OPPOSITE: Gilbert Stuart's 1797 portrait of George Washington, the first painting purchased for the White House, being reframed in 2004. After being hung in various rooms in the White House, it has been on view in the East Room since 1929.

term in the midst of the War of 1812 with Great Britain. In late August of 1814, six months before the war ended, British troops invaded the capital and set fire to several buildings, including the President's House. Though intrepid First Lady Dolley Madison famously rescued Gilbert Stuart's portrait of George Washington and important Cabinet papers before she fled the property, the house was completely gutted, requiring a massive reconstruction. President Madison oversaw the rebuilding effort with James Hoban, the original architect, and when James Monroe assumed office in 1817, he was tasked with the interiors, as most of the furnishings had been lost or destroyed. Also, in 1824, President Monroe built the South Portico (the North Portico was added by President Andrew Jackson in 1829–30). The porticoes were originally conceived by Hoban years before they were actually constructed; today it's impossible to imagine the building without them.

By the early 19th century, French style was all the rage, and President Monroe, a former U.S. ambassador to France, ardently embraced it, installing deep mahogany doorframes, elaborate plaster architectural ornamentation, rich Aubusson carpets, and elegant crystal chandeliers. Though he commissioned a suite of Federal-style chairs from a local Georgetown craftsman to furnish the East Room, in 1817 the president also authorized agents to purchase a 53-piece suite of gilded-beechwood furniture by Parisian cabinetmaker Pierre-Antoine Bellangé. The suite was bought for what is now the Blue Room, but the original upholstery was crimson satin emblazoned with olive branches. Monroe also purchased grand bronze-doré decorative objects in France, including an immense mirrored table plateau for the State Dining Room, mantel clocks, centerpieces, vases, and sculptural candelabra, many of which are still in use today.

It was during this time that Congress began to comprehend and appreciate the White House's role and public functions and authorized an additional $20,000 for it to be furnished in a style equal to its scale and grandeur. Monroe believed that the Executive Mansion—its official title until 1901, when President Theodore Roosevelt renamed it to avoid confusion with the residences of state governors—should be so magnificent as to hold its own with the palaces of the leaders of Europe. After Monroe invested close to this amount on the French furniture and objects alone, he subsequently received another $30,000 appropriation. (In 1826, not long after Monroe left office, Congress passed legislation mandating that to the best of each administration's ability, White House furniture should be crafted in the States, which resulted in a collection of French-influenced furnishings that were American-made.)

Though this appreciation for all things French would last for decades, in 1860, President

CLOCKWISE, FROM TOP LEFT: A Louis XVI–style armchair believed to be purchased by George Washington in the 1790s for the President's House in Philadelphia; it was acquired by the White House in 1963 as a result of First Lady Jacqueline Kennedy's restoration project. A sofa and two armchairs from a 53-piece suite of circa-1817 gilded furniture by Pierre-Antoine Bellangé, which was procured in Paris by President Monroe for the Oval Room (now the Blue Room) of the White House; President James Buchanan sold most of the suite in 1860. A mahogany armchair in the French style by Georgetown cabinetmaker William King, Jr., one of 28 pieces Monroe ordered for the East Room, where they were in use for more than five decades, until they were removed by President Ulysses S. Grant in 1873. The pier table from the original Bellangé suite, one of the few pieces of furniture that has remained in the White House continuously for more than two centuries; Mrs. Kennedy reportedly discovered it being used as a sawhorse in the White House woodshop in 1961. As a result of Mrs. Kennedy's restoration efforts, several Bellangé pieces have since been reacquired.

CLOCKWISE, FROM ABOVE: Thomas Birch's 1828 painting, *Mouth of the Delaware*. This porcelain and gilt-relief dessert cooler and soup tureen, part of a set made in 1806 by the Nast factory of Paris, were purchased by James Madison when he served as Thomas Jefferson's secretary of state and later used during Madison's presidency. In the East Room, a gilt-bronze candelabra, attributed to Pierre-Philippe Thomire, was a Monroe-era acquisition. A tall Federal-style case clock, circa 1795–1805, was crafted by John and Thomas Seymour of Boston; it has been a mainstay in the Oval Office through several administrations.

CLOCKWISE, FROM ABOVE: This early-19th-century gilt-bronze mantel clock, by Denière et Matelin of Paris, depicts Hannibal, the famed Carthaginian military commander. Charles-Honoré Lannuier's circa-1810 gueridon, of mahogany, satinwood, rosewood, and gilded brass with an intricate Italian-marble top, is one of the finest pieces by the celebrated cabinetmaker. An Empire-style mahogany sofa, with arms decorated with bronze sphinxes, is believed to have belonged to Dolley Madison; the sofa was placed in the Red Room during the Kennedy administration, when a distinctive scarlet silk was used for both the upholstery and the wall covering.

CLOCKWISE, FROM LEFT: A Queen Anne–style side chair and an armchair in the William and Mary style were made by A. H. Davenport for President Theodore Roosevelt's State Dining Room. This Rococo Revival center divan is from a suite purchased by Harriet Lane (the niece of President Buchanan, she served as his White House hostess); originally installed in the Blue Room, in recent years it was re-covered in red and placed in the China Room. A cushioned faux-bamboo side chair, dating from the 1870s, is from a suite made for the White House bedrooms. This 1890–92 landscape is one of eight Paul Cézanne paintings received in 1952 from a bequest to the White House by collector Charles A. Loeser. Though the Limoges-porcelain state dinnerware, ordered by First Lady Mary Todd Lincoln, was made in France by Haviland & Co., it was hand-painted in New York; President Abraham Lincoln considered its $3,200 cost to be a great extravagance, one of many incurred by his wife, but the china's aubergine border and painterly Great Seal were popular, and the service was replenished for many years, though few pieces remain today.

James Buchanan decided to sell most of Monroe's Bellangé suite at auction, replacing it with Victorian Rococo Revival pieces that were considered to be more stylish at the time. Sadly, from the entire suite, only a pier table remained within the Residence. Since 1961, when First Lady Jacqueline Kennedy initiated her White House restoration program and set out to reacquire as much of the Bellangé suite as possible (she reportedly rescued the abandoned pier table from a basement workshop, where it was being used as a sawhorse), original pieces have continued to be returned to the White House. The antiques have been supplemented by a group of reproductions commissioned by Mrs. Kennedy. A long-term project to restore and regild the Bellangé furniture, spearheaded by First Lady Laura Bush in 2005 and underway for more than a decade with the support and guidance of the White House Historical Association, was recently completed.

Over the years, as one administration gave way to the next, rooms changed functions and furnishings often came and went through sales and public auctions. It's shocking to realize that up until the turn of the century, White House furniture, decorative objects, and tableware were often sold if they were deemed to have fallen out of style or when a new president took office and redecorated to reflect a new administration's mindset— essentially throwing history to the wind, time after time.

The physical condition of the White House was of even greater concern. In 1833, President Andrew Jackson had running water installed (before that, water was drawn from a well and distributed throughout the building in buckets), and when Martin Van Buren took office four years later, he added rudimentary central heating, which was upgraded by President Franklin Pierce in 1853. But the house was never truly comfortable and was even considered rather unhealthy due to its damp basement and nearby swampland. As a child, I read about Abraham Lincoln's son Willie, who died in 1862 at age 11 from typhoid fever that was believed to have been contracted from polluted water piped to the White House from the Potomac River, water that had been contaminated by Union soldiers encamped on its banks. He died in an upstairs bedroom and was embalmed in the Green Room; after viewing his body there, his mother, First Lady Mary Todd Lincoln, apparently never stepped in the room again. There were also growing safety concerns, par-

ABOVE: Sterling-silver flatware in the Minuet pattern, made by the International Silver Company of Connecticut and engraved *President's House*, was selected by First Lady Grace Coolidge in 1926 and in use for the next five decades.

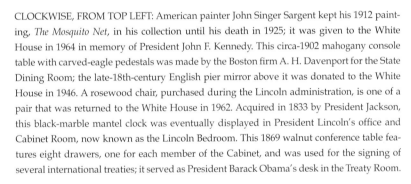

CLOCKWISE, FROM TOP LEFT: American painter John Singer Sargent kept his 1912 painting, *The Mosquito Net*, in his collection until his death in 1925; it was given to the White House in 1964 in memory of President John F. Kennedy. This circa-1902 mahogany console table with carved-eagle pedestals was made by the Boston firm A. H. Davenport for the State Dining Room; the late-18th-century English pier mirror above it was donated to the White House in 1946. A rosewood chair, purchased during the Lincoln administration, is one of a pair that was returned to the White House in 1962. Acquired in 1833 by President Jackson, this black-marble mantel clock was eventually displayed in President Lincoln's office and Cabinet Room, now known as the Lincoln Bedroom. This 1869 walnut conference table features eight drawers, one for each member of the Cabinet, and was used for the signing of several international treaties; it served as President Barack Obama's desk in the Treaty Room.

CLOCKWISE, FROM ABOVE: A rosewood center table, inlaid with satin-wood, holly, and boxwood marquetry, was crafted by Herter Brothers as part of the celebrated firm's 1875 redecoration of the Red Room, which was commissioned by First Lady Julia Grant. A gilded lady's chair by Herter Brothers, one of 11 pieces the firm made for the Red Room. An Andrew Wyeth watercolor landscape, *Mrs. Charlie Stone*, was painted in 1942; the artist's father and sister are also represented in the White House collection.

RIGHT: A 2007 painting by artist Peter Waddell depicts the decor of President Lincoln's office and Cabinet Room, located on the east side of the second floor of the White House; the space is now known as the Lincoln Bedroom. Lincoln signed the Emancipation Proclamation from the large wooden table shown in the painting, and it took effect on January 1, 1863, as the nation headed into its third year of war. BELOW: A color lithograph of the Lincoln family by Thomas Kelly of New York, depicting the president, First Lady Mary Todd Lincoln, and three of their four sons, from left, Tad, Robert, and Willie. Prints of the first family were very popular during the Lincoln administration, and this lithograph, in particular, has been on display in the Lincoln Sitting Room in the past.

ticularly after the conspiracy that resulted in the assassination of President Lincoln and si-
multaneous attempts to kill both Vice President Andrew Johnson and the secretary of state—
events that forever changed the perception of security for families living in the White House.

By 1869, the time of Ulysses S. Grant's presidency, the White House was no longer the largest—
or even one of the largest—houses in America. The end of the Civil War unleashed a period
of enormous wealth as the Industrial Revolution took hold, and the White House began to
seem modest compared to the grand residences commissioned by Gilded Age industrial-
ists. Mansions such as Biltmore House in Asheville, North Carolina, and Newport, Rhode
Island's Marble House and the Breakers were fitted out with historic revivalist details such

ABOVE: An early 1870s photograph of the Blue Room taken during the administration of Ulysses S. Grant. The room
had been decorated by President Andrew Johnson's daughter, Martha Johnson Patterson, during his administration
(1865–69), using rectilinear panels to contrast with the oval shape of the room.

as towers and turrets and comprised spaces for entertaining in the style of the day: smoking, billiard, and music rooms; greenhouses filled with orchids; and halls lined with tapestries and hunting trophies.

The occupants of the White House made every effort to keep up—and stay stylistically current. First Lady Julia Grant ordered furniture handcrafted by New York's Herter Brothers, then the height of fashion and considered to be the nation's leading cabinetmakers and interior design firm, boasting a client list that included some of America's wealthiest families, including the Vanderbilts and the Astors. By the time Chester A. Arthur became president in 1881, the popularity of the Aesthetic Movement was so strong that he hired Louis Comfort Tiffany—perhaps America's greatest exemplar of the style—to fill the White House with stained glass, carved and inlaid tables and cabinets, stenciled ceilings, richly patterned wallpapers and carpets, and dozens of potted palms. The opulent interiors were reflective of paintings by James McNeill Whistler and John Singer Sargent, the most sought after artists of the time.

The Gilded Age was undoubtedly when the White House was most thoroughly decorated in a unique, identifiable style. However, though President Arthur sold off 24 wagonloads of unwanted furnishings to help fund his design plans, even Tiffany had to work with many items preserved or left behind, incorporating them into his schemes. Something that I would very much come to realize was that the White House has never been a place for a single, overarching aesthetic, largely due to the limitations of time—four-year stints do not allow you to do complete and thorough renovations. Also, out of practicality as well as respect for what has come before, a wholesale clearing out by new occupants would be considered as inappropriate as it would be difficult. There is ultimately something very American about adapting and reusing, not to mention the constant budget concerns that are always top of mind for each president.

By the end of the 19th century, as the country and the scale of the government required to manage it grew, the White House became too small to encompass both family living quarters and the presidential workplace. Plans for an expansion were developed during the administrations of both President Benjamin Harrison and William McKinley, but they never came to fruition. After McKinley's assassination, President Theodore Roosevelt finally took matters in hand and in 1902 hired Charles Follen McKim, of the preeminent Gilded Age architectural firm McKim, Mead & White, to deal with the troubled, overcrowded building.

McKim's first decision was to relegate most of the administrative operations from the Residence to a new building conceived as the Temporary Executive Office Building (though

ABOVE: The Blue Room during the Chester A. Arthur administration, one of several rooms the president commissioned Louis Comfort Tiffany to redecorate in 1882. After complaining that the White House looked like "a badly kept barracks," President Arthur sold off 24 wagonloads of existing furniture and objects to fund his opulent Victorian design schemes. In the Blue Room, Tiffany used a range of robin's-egg blues on the walls and added an intricate ivory-and-silver frieze of embossed, hand-pressed paper. RIGHT: The Gilded Age version of the East Room, after its 1873 redecoration by President Grant, included the construction of two beams supported by gilded white columns. The ceiling between the beams was painted blue and blush pink, and walls were clad in gray and gold patterned wallpapers; new mantels and mirrors and a fleet of ornate gas chandeliers were installed as well.

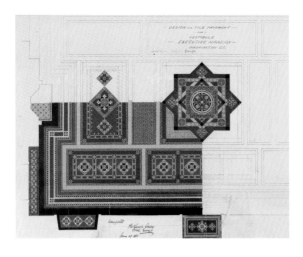

CLOCKWISE, FROM TOP LEFT: A drawing for an encaustic-tile floor laid in the Entrance Hall in 1880, a project begun during the Grant administration that was finished under President Rutherford B. Hayes; the floor was removed two decades later, during the Theodore Roosevelt renovation. Artist Peter Waddell's 2006 painting of the circa-1891 Entrance Hall depicts the lighting of a gas lamp on the interior side of the Louis Comfort Tiffany stained-glass screen; President Arthur had requested a screen to make the space more welcoming—and literally warmer, as it was designed to shield guests in the drawing rooms from cold winter air gusting through the front door. An 1889 photograph of the Entrance Hall, taken during the Benjamin Harrison administration.

never intended to be a permanent structure, it now encompasses the West Wing). A maze of Victorian flower and fruit conservatories, which had proliferated to such an extent that some critics claimed the president's home had become Washington's premier florist, were demolished to make room. The architect then oversaw a serious renovation of the Residence—replacing most wood beams with steel, upgrading warped floorboards with wood and stone floors, and stripping the interiors of stenciling, stained glass, and architectural flourishes added by previous administrations. The functions of several rooms, even entire floors, changed: The basement became a finished ground floor, with a proper entrance leading from a new semicircular drive; bathrooms for visitors were moved downstairs from the State Floor; staff rooms were carved out of the attic; and the entire second floor was designated as the presidential family quarters. (The president still kept a private office on this floor, as the official Oval Office in the Executive Office Building wasn't designed until 1909, for President William Howard Taft.)

Roosevelt's impressive new Entrance Hall perhaps best reflected McKim's bold transfor-

ABOVE: A hand-tinted photo of the Entrance Hall in 1904, following the major renovation undertaken by President Theodore Roosevelt, who hired Charles Follen McKim, of the preeminent Gilded Age architectural firm McKim, Mead & White. The architect was tasked with restoring the classical essence of the White House while creating a sense of grandeur befitting its role as a symbol of American power and supremacy. The ornament and pattern of prior decades were stripped away, replaced by neoclassical columns, monumental gilded mirrors, and wide expanses of limestone floors.

mation, showcasing monumental Doric columns, neoclassical architectural detail, massive gilded mirrors, streamlined benches, and floors paved with Illinois limestone. McKim had reimagined the building to reflect the aesthetic of a new president at the dawn of a new century, restoring the structure to its classical essence and endowing it with the grandeur most of us associate with the White House today. Yet once again, the house fell victim to criticism, with a refrain that the house was too palatial and European in style, and far too identifiable with grand municipal buildings, such as the city's majestic Union Station. And in retrospect, the renovation that McKim described as a "nip and tuck" caused major structural weaknesses that deteriorated over time, contributing to a near disaster that wouldn't become apparent until almost a half century had passed.

Two decades later, in the mid-1920s, First Lady Grace Coolidge assembled an official White House advisory committee of antiques experts and collectors and initiated federal legislation authorizing the acceptance of gifts to help procure historic furnishings for the State Rooms. She also oversaw a massive renovation to transform the attic and roof of the Residence into a third floor that comprised additional guest rooms, storage areas, offices, and a solarium. Unfortunately, the construction work was rushed on an accelerated schedule and poorly engineered, and, more important, the weight of the added rooms wasn't properly supported, exacerbating the structural flaws created during the McKim renovation. Unknowingly, the renovation caused the building to be seriously—and dangerously—destabilized.

The White House was by now a repository of history, but its jumble of furniture styles and the range of quality reflected in its collection was rather prosaic. Plus, the nationwide popularity of the Colonial Revival style meant that department-store copies of antiques began to fill not only America's living rooms, but also the rooms of the White House. In fact, after a 1948–52 structural renovation overseen by President Harry S. Truman, the president and his wife, Bess, had hired Charles Haight, an interior designer from the New York retailer B. Altman & Co., to handle their interior decoration. B. Altman had offered to warehouse the building's existing furnishings during the construction period, and then provide the redecoration at cost. With their modest budget allocation in mind, the Trumans accepted the offer, though critics later decried the interiors as generic and institutional. (I loved reading that when President Truman gave former First Lady Eleanor Roosevelt a tour of the newly redecorated rooms, it was reported that she graciously told him they were lovely, but privately confided to friends that they looked "exactly like a Sheraton Hotel.")

As the public rooms became more homogenized and watered-down historic, the private

NOTE: The images featured on these two pages are circa-1904 hand-colored platinum prints by the Detroit Photographic Company featuring the State Dining Room and the three parlors on the State Floor. ABOVE: The State Dining Room during Theodore Roosevelt's administration, after the 1902 renovation by McKim, Mead & White. The walls were paneled in oak and featured a heavily carved cornice mounted with large hunting trophies, including the heads of deer and moose. Green velvet upholstery and window treatments were designed to coordinate with sumptuous 16th-century Flemish tapestries, and the room was lit with electrified silver-plated fixtures. LEFT: Architect Charles McKim restored the elegant Empire-style decor of the Blue Room, commissioning a suite of furniture inspired by the original Monroe-era French chairs by Bellangé and upholstering the walls in a custom-woven, deep-blue ribbed silk.

RIGHT: During the Roosevelt renovation, the walls of the Green Room were covered in a lustrous green silk, and McKim installed a white marble mantel he relocated from the State Dining Room. BELOW: McKim replaced the Red Room's exuberant pattern, ornament, and ornate furnishings with small-scale, refined tables and seating in classic silhouettes. The upholstery and walls were covered in a rich red fabric, which set off a collection of portraits in ornate gilded frames, including Gilbert Stuart's life-size portrait of George Washington, which was displayed over the fireplace.

ABOVE: An elevation of the White House showing the East and West Wings. President Theodore Roosevelt masterminded the construction of the West Wing to relocate staff and administrative functions from the second floor of the Residence. BELOW: An 1899 photograph showing the maze of greenhouses west of the White House that proliferated between 1857 and the turn of the century; they were razed in 1902 to make room for the new executive offices. OPPOSITE, FROM TOP: Architect Charles McKim designed the new East Entrance, creating a proper guest entry that one accessed from a graceful semicircular drive.

quarters became even more evocative of mainstream taste. In 1947, President Truman forcefully lobbied to install a controversial balcony atop the South Portico, creating a private place to enjoy what he termed the "best view in the White House." It's a spot that was very popular with subsequent first families and much beloved by the Obamas and their children. In a house that is essentially hermetically sealed, it is one of the few places where you can actually feel that you're outdoors. Though, I recall we couldn't open the door that leads to the balcony from the Yellow Oval Room without first alerting the Secret Service. (Understandably, unexpected movements are not welcomed by the diligent security team.) Once you're outside, sitting on the balcony feels almost like being on the porch of a regular house, looking out over a classic American lawn—albeit one that's punctuated by the Washington Monument.

It was during the Truman administration that the building underwent the most drastic structural overhaul since it had been torched by the British army in 1814. Truman often joked that the White House creaked so much, and its chandeliers swayed so often, that it must be inhabited by ghosts. In truth, President Franklin D. Roosevelt, likely preoccupied by wartime demands,

OPPOSITE: A 1950 photograph of the gutted White House interior during the Truman renovation, which lasted from 1948 to 1952. The open construction area measured 165 feet long, 85 feet wide, and nearly 80 feet tall. I remember finding this picture in a book when I was a kid, and I couldn't comprehend that there were a bulldozer and a dump truck inside the White House. ABOVE: After the East Room ceiling began to collapse in 1948, during President Harry S. Truman's administration, wood bracing was installed until the renovation could begin.

had dismissed a 1941 report from the Army Corps of Engineers that found the building in dire need of repair. Then, in the summer of 1948, near the end of Truman's first term, one leg of his daughter Margaret's piano broke through the second floor and the ceiling below, and it was no longer possible to ignore the fact that the building was structurally unsound and in great danger of collapsing. (Following a thorough investigation, a buildings commissioner announced that the ceiling beams "are staying up there from force of habit only.")

However, Truman, campaigning for reelection and fearing headlines comparing a collapsing White House with the state of his own administration, postponed the renovation until later in the year. It was nearly too late, as in October the ceiling in the East Room began to cave in and required extensive bracing. After he won reelection, the president and his family moved across the street to Blair House, the presidential guest quarters, for nearly four years while the White House was gutted to its frame and backhoes arrived to excavate deep into the ground. Years ago, as a kid, I remember seeing a picture-book photo of a bulldozer in the middle of a demolished White House that has always stuck in my mind. It was unsettling and unimaginable at the time, the idea that something so emblematic of America—something that was so unquestionably permanent—could appear so vulnerable.

Only the roof, the third floor, and the original stone walls from the 1790s and the post-fire

OPPOSITE: The East Room in 1950, being dismantled prior to the demolition; the paneling and millwork were meticulously labeled and preserved to be reinstalled post-renovation. ABOVE: Photographer Abbie Rowe, of the National Park Service, documented the entire White House renovation project, including this dramatic image of the demolished interior space. A towering steel framework was constructed to support the third floor and the roof while the remaining floors were demolished and a new basement was dug. LEFT: The limestone floor in the Entrance Hall was removed and cataloged for storage in late 1949.

OPPOSITE: What is now known as the Yellow Oval Room, with the north wall and part of the floor removed to allow the installation of steel shoring columns, exposing the oval Blue Room beneath. CLOCKWISE, FROM TOP LEFT: The north wall of the Blue Room after the brick walls were stripped of their plaster and the door-frames leading to the Red Room (*left*), the Cross Hall, and the Green Room (*right*) were removed. Though President and Mrs. Truman were chided by critics for their budget-conscious decision to commission interior designers from the department store B. Altman & Co. to decorate the post-renovation interiors, the team was overseen by Charles T. Haight, a highly respected Parsons School of Design–trained talent; the team used a deep-blue silk damask by Schumacher for the Blue Room wall covering. The Blue Room in the summer of 1952, after the renovation project had been completed and all of the furnishings were installed.

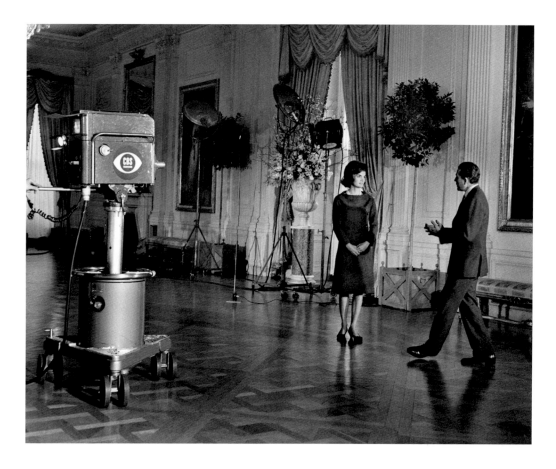

restoration were left in place, creating a one-million-cubic-foot hollow area that measured 165 feet long, 85 feet wide, and nearly 80 feet high. Interior materials and architectural details were meticulously salvaged, labeled for reuse, and warehoused, though, due to time and budget limitations, much of this ended up sold off in souvenir kits or discarded to landfill. Hundreds of tons of concrete and steel replaced the building's foundation and cracked wooden supports. Plaster-finished interior walls and new windows were installed; wood paneling, millwork, and architectural details were restored or replaced with new iterations; floors were relaid and refinished; and the latest electrical, plumbing, heating, and air-conditioning systems were put in place, as well as up-to-date communications networks. Additional elevators were installed and a basement with two subterranean levels was dug out, making room for storage and mechanical systems, with contiguous space for carpentry and florist workshops, quarters for the gardening staff, and more.

Though the Truman structural reconstruction was monumental, costing millions of dollars, the most obvious and visual transformation of the White House occurred during President John F. Kennedy's administration. It was not only because it was featured so

ABOVE: Jacqueline Kennedy with CBS correspondent Charles Collingwood in the East Room filming her groundbreaking televised tour of the White House, which aired February 14, 1962. The first lady's TV special was syndicated worldwide and seen by 80 million viewers; the first night it was broadcast, it was watched by nearly one-third of the country.

prominently on the relatively new medium of television—Jacqueline Kennedy's ground-breaking personal tour was filmed as a TV special seen by 80 million viewers on all three major networks and syndicated worldwide—but also because it brought well-deserved attention to the history, beauty, and majesty of the White House, establishing an iconic memory for generations to come.

With the energy and enthusiasm of a 31-year-old with a keen interest in culture, decorative arts, and history, and a lifelong appreciation for beautiful houses owned by the wealthy and influential, Mrs. Kennedy was ideally suited to her restoration project. Most import-ant, the first lady understood that in order to elevate the image of the White House yet also live within its walls as a family, there must be a well-defined separation between the public rooms and the upstairs private quarters—something she achieved by installing a family dining room and small kitchen on the second floor. Working with Mrs. Henry Parish II, known as "Sister," of Parish-Hadley Associates, and, subsequently, Stéphane Boudin, of the French decorating firm Maison Jansen, and selecting philanthropist Henry Francis du Pont, the definitive American furniture and decorative-arts collector, as one of her advisors, the first lady undertook a campaign to restore the historical gravitas of the building while adding warmth and grace to rooms she considered to be stately but shockingly shabby.

Included in *Sister*, the wonderful biography of Sister Parish written by her daughter and granddaughter, is a first-person account of Mrs. Parish stubbornly driving herself through a blinding snowstorm to get to Washington the day before President Kennedy's inaugura-tion. I loved that she was so single-minded in her mission to deliver her three blue duffel bags of swatches to Mrs. Kennedy that she remained undaunted by what turned out to be a harrowing, nearly 20-hour trip as the blizzard paralyzed the East Coast. She also mentions that despite being a fervent old-school Republican, she was thrilled to be at the inaugura-tion: "I certainly wasn't feeling Republican or Democrat or anything but a proud American that day," she wrote. "All any of us felt was exaltation." Mrs. Parish—armed with her extensive Rolodex of generous friends and clients and soliciting donations along with the first lady—laid the groundwork for the elegant redecoration of the State Rooms and trans-formed the private quarters into a warm, inviting home for the young family, though they apparently ran through the entire decorating-budget allocation of $50,000 within the first two weeks, having spent it all on the upstairs spaces for the family.

Eventually Mrs. Parish was dismissed, reprimanded by Mrs. Kennedy for ordering a rug from France, even though it had been preapproved as in keeping with plans to return the

White House to its original state. Mrs. Parish later admitted to learning that the first lady had been told that she had kicked young Caroline—a rumor the decorator didn't exactly confirm or deny. The continuation of the decoration and restoration project was subsequently taken over by Henry du Pont and Boudin, an interior designer introduced to Mrs. Kennedy by her friend Jayne Wrightsman, an esteemed philanthropist, collector, and Francophile.

Jackie Kennedy inherited a true mixed bag of furniture and objects for the public rooms, and both she and the president were shocked to learn that little existed that had been there for more than a dozen years. Early on, she made it a large part of her mission to ensure that the interiors of the White House would reflect the beauty, integrity, and character of the building itself—as well as serve as an appropriate setting for the cultural and social events she planned on behalf of the administration. It was also important to her to represent the first families who had lived in the mansion during its 161 years and she hoped to entice collectors of Americana to donate historic furnishings that had previously been sold or given away. In a 1961 *Life* magazine interview, she told journalist Hugh Sidey, "Everything in the White House must have a reason for being there."

The first lady's visionary efforts spearheaded the passage of a powerful federal law that named the furniture, fixtures, and decorative objects of the White House as its inalienable property, thus preventing the future sale or deaccession of any furnishings and protecting the interiors of what is essentially the most revered building in America. Never again would history be so casually discarded. Banishing the worn department-store reproductions to storage, she solicited gifts of period textiles, furniture, and art through her newly created Fine

Arts Committee, which was later officially renamed the Committee for the Preservation of the White House. This group has served a vital role for decades and continues to vet and approve all gifts to the collection.

As Mrs. Kennedy and her committee began to track down furniture with a connection to the White House that had been given away or sold—as well as antiques that fit within the aesthetic direction for each historic room—she and her newly hired curator, Lorraine Pearce, scoured the entire building to assess its contents, soon discovering a stash of silver-gilt flatware that President Monroe ordered from France on a storage room shelf. The celebrated Resolute desk was installed in President Kennedy's Oval Office after the first lady found it under a pile of electronics in the broadcast room. A present from Queen Victoria to Rutherford B. Hayes in 1880, the desk had been used in the private offices of 14 consecutive presidents until it was relegated to the broadcast studio after the Truman reconstruction. And a scouting visit to a down-

OPPOSITE: Mrs. Kennedy examines a set of blueprints with Lorraine Pearce, the White House curator, in July 1961. ABOVE: The first lady on the cover of the September 1, 1961, issue of *Life* magazine; in the accompanying feature that described her restoration project, she told journalist Hugh Sidey, "Everything in the White House must have a reason for being there."

THE WHITE HOUSE
WASHINGTON

Dear Sister —

You mentioned Leleu commode
at Connoisseur — what I liked was
the Weisweiler small table — light
& dark wood — for between bergeres.
That is such a prominent spot I know
D'Alva one will look awful

Weis. is so pure & lovely — Couldn't
you browbeat Mrs C. So she gets it
to our price range — about $6 or $800
or she could take it as a tax
deduction (We won't announce it but

don't tell her that) —
Tell her it will be in guide — in
your book in book David Douglas
Duncan is doing on W.H. — like his
Kremlin one — And in her book she could
have it marked as W.H. collection —
which I think people should begin to
be proud of & make sacrifices for —

His is $22 which is absurd — but
I thought that angle might
interest her & if you could do that it
would be fantastic

See you Wednesday
love Jackie

ABOVE AND RIGHT: A letter from Jacqueline Kennedy to Mrs. Henry Parish II — known as "Sister" — the well-respected interior designer who masterminded the decoration of the family's private quarters and was highly instrumental in the initial stages of the restoration project. Reporters were confused when the news was released that the new president and first lady had selected Sister Parish as their designer, with one headline famously announcing, "Kennedys Pick Nun to Decorate White House." OPPOSITE: Mrs. Parish's notes and swatches for the Kennedys' Yellow Oval Room and Family Dining Room.

THE WHITE HOUSE

WASHINGTON, D.C.

MAIL EARLY

US AIR MAIL 7¢

AIR MAIL

Mrs Henry Parish II
22 E 69th St
New York City

stairs men's room landed a trove of marble busts, including one of George Washington, all more than a century old.

Then, remarkable furnishings started arriving as a result of Sister Parish's outreach and the first lady's personal requests—contributing to the restoration and decoration project had become a serious honor. Frances and John Loeb, noted collectors of French Impressionists and friends of Mrs. Parish, agreed to restore the Yellow Oval Room, Mrs. Kennedy's favorite room in the White House, and Jayne Wrightsman donated a beautiful 18th-century French desk for the space as well. Sister Parish and her husband, Henry, gave a Lincoln-era Victorian settee and two matching chairs, and as a few gilded pieces from James Monroe's Bellangé collection started to make their way back to the White House, former ambassador to France and Secretary of the Treasury C. Douglas Dillon contributed a selection of American Empire furniture, including a sofa attributed to Dolley Madison. Kennedy loyalist Averell Harriman and his wife, Marie, gave a Whistler painting—one which would assume a special importance on the night of the Obama inauguration—and when several large panels of antique French wallpaper representing Revolutionary War scenes were discovered in a London antiques shop and deemed perfect for the Kennedy family dining room, the philanthropist Brooke Astor, a family friend, purchased them as a donation.

Captivated by the charm of this intelligent, energetic president and his first lady, people

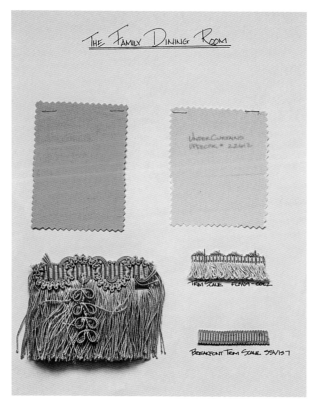

ABOVE: Jacqueline Kennedy's Master Bedroom, which was decorated by Sister Parish. A daisy-print cotton by Dek Tillett was used for the curtains and headboard and a pale-green silk for the *lit à la couronne* canopy; one of the side-by-side mattresses was of firm horsehair to accommodate the president's back condition. LEFT: The sofa in the sitting area was slipcovered in white matelassé and paired with a mix of Louis XV– and Louis XVI–style chairs. The mantel, installed during the 1951 Truman renovation, bore a plaque noting that Abraham Lincoln slept in the room during the time he served as president. In 1963, as Mrs. Kennedy was moving her young family to temporary living quarters after President Kennedy's assassination, she asked that a similar plaque be added to the mantel, stating "In this room lived John Fitzgerald Kennedy with his wife Jacqueline—during the two years ten months and 2 days he was president of the United States. January 20 1961–November 22 1963." Though during the Nixon administration the mantel was put in storage in favor of the current, more historically relevant, circa-1816 piece from a Benjamin Latrobe–designed house, a duplicate plaque was affixed to the 19th-century mantel in President Kennedy's adjacent bedroom, which remains in place today.

RIGHT AND BELOW: President Kennedy's bedroom, which featured a stately four-poster. The president chose a blue-and-white toile with an angel motif for the window curtains and bed canopy, telling Mrs. Parish that he had "always loved angels." The 18th-century Philadelphia tall chest in the president's sitting area was the first significant donation of fine furniture to the restoration project; a painting by Childe Hassam, *Allies Day, May 1917* (one of two Hassam works in this room), is displayed above. The Obamas used this space as their Family Sitting Room, and we placed this tall chest adjacent to the window wall. President Obama installed Hassam's *The Avenue in the Rain* (not shown) in his Oval Office.

RIGHT: The Yellow Oval Room, used by several previous presidents as a private study, was transformed by Mrs. Kennedy into an elegant formal drawing room for the first family; the windows face south, with views of the Washington Monument, and the door at right led to President Kennedy's bedroom. Though Mrs. Parish spearheaded a campaign to request furnishings and funding for the entire restoration project, this room, in particular, was Mrs. Kennedy's favorite, and its decor was the result of a combined effort between the first lady, her friend Jayne Wrightsman (who was a true Francophile), Sister Parish, and Stéphane Boudin—the head of Paris design firm Maison Jansen. Mrs. Parish convinced her friends Frances and John Loeb to underwrite the cost of the room's decoration, including furniture and draperies designed by Boudin, whom she considered a rival. When it was finished, the room reflected the Louis XVI refinement of the Madison- and Monroe-era White House, an aesthetic Mrs. Kennedy decided should be the definitive, overriding influence in the restoration of every room.

were inspired to be extraordinarily generous. Reading through the accounts of all of the various donations and contributions, I realized that it was a surprisingly bipartisan effort. Sadly, though Mrs. Kennedy had a long, thoughtful wish list to complete her task of revitalizing the White House, she would never obtain all the things she hoped to secure for the interiors; her role as first lady was tragically cut short barely a thousand days into their tenure.

As I worked with the Obamas on the project, I was able to identify certain elements from Mrs. Kennedy's original plans for the Yellow Oval Room that were still missing and that she had been unable to procure. Out of respect for her vision and so inspired by the idea of continuing her design scheme for the space—her favorite, and to me, the room that remains the most Jackie-influenced—my partner, James, and I gave a set of Louis XVI chairs to be used at the dining table that overlooks the South Lawn, as well as a large Oushak rug that was both appropriate for the space and well suited to her original color palette.

In all my research, the Kennedy years were the ones that inspired me the most. It was an era that reflected the worldly sophistication and elegance of a forward-minded president and his young family, but most important, it was the time when America realized that the White House was an institution that deserved to be honored and protected, that the history of it was of extraordinary importance to the country. Being known as the People's House, it was expected that it would not only be filled with an exceptional collection of historic furniture and objects, but that it would also be a place infused with life and energy. There would always be an emphasis on the best of America and celebrating excellence in both art and culture, and it would serve as the setting for exciting, historic social events—dinner parties, concerts and performances, receptions and State Dinners that would welcome artists, musicians, scientists, and great creative minds and thought leaders from all over the world. The Kennedys also promoted cultural life beyond the White House, as the first lady famously convinced André Malraux, the French minister of culture, to loan Leonardo da Vinci's *Mona Lisa* for an exhibition at Washington's National Gallery and the Metropolitan Museum of Art in New York.

OPPOSITE: President Kennedy in the Oval Office in February 1962, seated at the celebrated carved-oak Resolute desk, crafted from the timbers of the HMS *Resolute* and a gift from Queen Victoria to Rutherford B. Hayes in 1880. Though the desk had been used by 14 presidents, after the Truman Reconstruction it was relegated to the broadcast room, where it was discovered by Mrs. Kennedy. Sister Parish had decorated the space with Mrs. Kennedy in early 1961, retaining the Truman-era green carpet and draperies but adding nautical touches, including ship models and seascapes, to reflect the president's love of the sea and youthful mindset. A redecoration of the space by Stéphane Boudin, featuring a deep red carpet and streamlined white curtains trimmed in red, was installed on November 22, 1963, while the Kennedys were campaigning in Texas; it was never seen by the president or first lady. After the assassination, the president's personal items were removed before Mrs. Kennedy had a chance to view the completed room; she eventually decided against including a reproduction of the Oval Office at the John F. Kennedy Library in Boston.

This legacy was something that deeply resonated with the Obamas. It fit so naturally with their sense of curiosity, their fascination with and great appreciation for culture and the arts, and their open-minded embrace of the world at large. Though the Kennedys had established the archetype for the White House decorative style—a combination of different influences, held together by a James Monroe–period ideal—subsequent administrations added to the White House collection, carried on the restoration of the State Rooms, and updated the family quarters as needed. I realized that I could help the Obamas make the strongest personal impact, particularly in their private quarters, by adding iconic contemporary art to those monumental spaces. It was a way to counterbalance the sense of history—if not to wake a sleeping beauty, it was certainly a way to shake it up. And not since the Kennedys has there been a family that has had such a trailblazing, transformative effect on the White House.

Throughout the decades that followed the sixties, the White House remained a fixed ideal etched into the public perception and imagination. While working on this project, I needed to take all of this history into consideration to try to understand what was true and authentic about the building, what was myth, what was legend, and what myths and legends were so powerful that they might as well be true. My efforts had to be accomplished quickly and pragmatically. And these efforts, in turn, would likely be undone in another four or eight years.

Also, every aesthetic decision I made had to be considered through the prism of the mandate that Michelle Obama had given me: "How would this work for the next family?" She had a deep concern for the care and comfort of not only her family, but also for the first families that would follow, as well as a keen sense that she and her husband were custodians of this house for just a short period of time. Any potential changes should be respectful of both its past and its future.

The president made it clear early on that he intended to have a private dinner with his family every night that he was in Washington. But making a family home in what is in a very real sense a national monument—creating warmth and comfort where world leaders, diplomats, reporters, senators, and congressmen all mingle; where the requirements of security were a constant factor; where privacy was at a premium and downtime was virtually nonexistent—was never going to be easy. I was very mindful that my primary purpose was to help make it possible for the Obamas, when they were not performing the multitude of duties required of each of them on any given day, to have a family life that was as normal and as balanced as possible.

RIGHT: The second-floor Center Hall, looking east, in 1962. Mrs. Kennedy positioned two halves of a coromandel screen to flank the door leading to the Grand Staircase, and Sister Parish grouped sofas and chairs to create a sense of intimacy in the voluminous space; the walls were lined with George Catlin's paintings of Native Americans and the western frontier. BELOW: The Treaty Room during the Kennedy Administration, with portraits of Presidents Zachary Taylor (*left*) and Andrew Johnson. The first lady transformed a second-floor parlor formerly known as the Monroe Room into a reception area that could serve as an after-hours conference room for the president. It was named the Treaty Room in honor of the important documents that had been signed within, including the Spanish-American peace protocol of 1898. Stéphane Boudin covered the walls with a deep-green velvetlike paper accented with a graphic geometric border motif inspired by the State Rooms of the Andrew Johnson–era White House.

LEFT: The Green Room in 1961, before its revamp by Boudin; the wall covering and draperies are a Robert Adam–inspired silk damask from the Truman era, and the portrait is of President Franklin Pierce. When it was finished, the Green Room—the first State Room to be furnished by the newly formed Fine Arts Committee and a collaboration between Boudin and Henry du Pont—was reportedly President Kennedy's favorite of the State Rooms. BELOW: The circa-1963 Blue Room, after its completion by designer Stéphane Boudin; the decoration was underwritten by Jayne and Charles Wrightsman, longtime Maison Jansen clients. Though Boudin's design was beloved by the first lady, it was considered highly controversial by critics at the time, as it was a distinct departure from the past. The elliptical room is challenging, as it comprises three windows, a fireplace, and five unevenly spaced doorways. Boudin unified the space with cream-on-cream striped walls and curtains of blue silk taffeta, with valances that continued around the room like a frieze; he also lined new reproductions of the Monroe-era Bellangé chairs around the perimeter and added a center table.

ABOVE AND LEFT: Stéphane Boudin's 1962 redesign of the Red Room, which evoked the French Empire style of Château de Malmaison, the country house of Empress Joséphine and Napoleon; Boudin had previously worked on the restoration of the château. Paintings were hung at both eye level and over the doorframes (the first lady explained that the pictures were hung high up on the wall to "relieve some of the redness of the room"), the gilt-wood chandelier was 1820s French, and the furniture included a Dolley Madison-era sofa and an exquisite Charles-Honoré Lannuier table topped with inlaid marble; the window treatments—gilded rods from which fell straight panels of cerise silk—were a Boudin signature.

ABOVE: A 1963 photograph of the indoor swimming pool in the West Wing, which had been installed by President Franklin Roosevelt in the West Terrace between the Residence and the West Wing so he could swim as therapy for his polio condition. The pool's mural, featuring scenes of the U.S. Virgin Islands, was provided by President Kennedy's father, Joseph P. Kennedy, and completed in 1962. Seven years later, President Nixon built a press room over the space to accommodate the growing White House press corps, and President Gerald R. Ford installed an outdoor pool and cabana in 1975. RIGHT: With the help of Sister Parish, Mrs. Kennedy transformed a former bedroom suite on the second floor into a small kitchen and President's Dining Room, establishing for the first time a completely separate private apartment for the Kennedys and subsequent first families. (Prior to this, meals were taken in the Family Dining Room on the State Floor.) Though the circa-1853 wallpaper was French, it received Henry du Pont's approval because it depicted Revolutionary War scenes; it had been discovered in a London antiques shop and was purchased and donated by Brooke Astor, a client of Mrs. Parish.

OPPOSITE: First Lady Lady Bird Johnson in the Center Hall on May 8, 1968, dressed for a gala dinner in honor of Prime Minister Thanom Kittikachorn of Thailand. RIGHT: President Lyndon Johnson and his family celebrating Christmas in the Yellow Oval Room on December 24, 1968, a few weeks before Richard M. Nixon was inaugurated; from left, Luci Johnson Nugent, Lyn Nugent, the first lady, President Johnson, Lynda Johnson Robb, and Lucinda Robb. BELOW: In the spring of 1968, members of President Johnson's staff watch breaking news on a bank of television sets in the Oval Office.

ABOVE: The Nixon family having dinner in the President's Dining Room; from left, First Lady Pat Nixon, Tricia Nixon, President Richard Nixon, David Eisenhower, and Julie Nixon Eisenhower. BELOW: First Lady Betty Ford in the East Room in August 1976, dancing with singer Tony Orlando at a State Dinner honoring President Urho Kekkonen of Finland. OPPOSITE, FROM TOP: Mrs. Ford (*right*) sharing lunch in the third-floor Solarium with Happy Rockefeller, wife of New York Governor Nelson Rockefeller, on August 22, 1974; President Gerald R. Ford had just named Governor Rockefeller incoming vice president. The Yellow Oval Room in October 1974, during the Ford administration, two months after President Ford assumed office following President Nixon's historic resignation.

ABOVE: The Master Bedroom in 1981, designed by Ted Graber for President and Mrs. Ronald Reagan; the hand-painted wallpaper was by Charles R. Gracie & Sons. LEFT: The president and First Lady Nancy Reagan meeting with Prince Charles and Princess Diana in the West Sitting Hall on November 9, 1985; a State Dinner in their honor was held later that evening.

RIGHT: President Reagan used the room next to the Master Bedroom as his President's Study (this later served as the Obamas' Family Sitting Room). The first family furnished the room with personal pieces, augmented by art and a few antiques from the White House collection; the overmantel painting is *Boy Fishing*, by Lila Cabot Perry, which is flanked by works by George Catlin, all of which were on loan from the National Gallery. BELOW: President George H. W. Bush in the Treaty Room on February 21, 1991, meeting with advisors to discuss the U.S. response to the Soviet peace plan with Iraq.

ABOVE: President Bill Clinton and First Lady Hillary Clinton collaborated with Little Rock, Arkansas–based designer Kaki Hockersmith on the interiors for their administration. The president's circa-1995 Oval Office featured sofas slipcovered in a bright awning stripe and a Prussian-blue rug with a prominent presidential seal at its center; Rembrandt Peale's circa-1823 portrait of President George Washington was displayed above the mantel, and a late-18th-century case clock stood by the door leading to the West Colonnade. LEFT: The walls of President Clinton's Treaty Room were a deep red, and its red linen curtains were topped with elaborate swagged valances.

LEFT: Several furniture pieces from the White House collection were incorporated by Fort Worth, Texas, designer Ken Blasingame in his sophisticated redesign of the George W. Bush family's Center Hall—some updated with stylish details like the tiger-stripe velvet covering the settee and chair seats. BELOW: In the President's Dining Room, Blasingame re-covered the Clinton-era dining chairs and installed a subtle damask fabric wall covering, against which President and Mrs. Bush displayed Georgia O'Keeffe's 1932 painting *Jimson Weed*.

LEFT: The Queens' Bedroom, named for the royals who have been guests of the White House, photographed during the Clinton era; this room and the Lincoln Bedroom are part of the second floor's family quarters, but they are primarily reserved for visiting dignitaries. (When President Obama invited me to stay over during his last year in office, this was the room I chose.) The room is furnished with New England Federal pieces and a carved American Sheraton tester bed. BELOW: The Lincoln Bedroom during the administration of George W. Bush. Formerly an office used by Lincoln and successive presidents, it was reconfigured as a bedroom during the 1902 Roosevelt renovation and features the Lincoln Bed; though purchased by Mrs. Lincoln, the bed was likely never used by her husband. Furnished during the Truman administration to evoke the 1860s, it was redone in 2005 by First Lady Laura Bush, who re-created the period details of Lincoln's original office, including its ornate window cornices. OPPOSITE: The Queens' Sitting Room in 2000, which still retains the decor installed by Mrs. Kennedy in the early '60s, including the neoclassical-style fabric used for the walls, curtains, and upholstery, as well as its gilded lacquer chest and table.

3   A NEW DAY

On the bitter-cold morning of Tuesday, January 20, 2009, under an icy blue sky, Barack Hussein Obama was sworn in as America's 44th president, filling the streets of Washington with millions of well-wishers and inspiring the largest crowd in inaugural history with his electrifying words. Meanwhile, I was inside the White House, trying to catch as much of his eloquence as I could from a TV perched in the corner of one room while I raced around, helping to orchestrate a small army of nearly 100 workers—housekeepers, butlers, carpenters, painters, florists, and support staff—as they swiftly cleaned the second and third floors, unpacked boxes, stocked the kitchen, moved furniture, hung paintings, and installed clothes in newly emptied closets. (Even more than a decade later, I think I've watched President Obama's inauguration ceremony—which included performances by Yo-Yo Ma and Aretha Franklin; a reading by poet Elizabeth Alexander, who has since become a good friend; and the president's historic speech—only in piecemeal fashion.)

If nothing, it was carefully choreographed chaos. I had been in planning mode for the previ-

ous month, making a few visits to meet with Mrs. Obama at the Hay-Adams hotel, where the family had moved after the holidays in order for the girls to start school. But by tradition we could not gain access to the Residence until 11 A.M. on Inauguration Day, after outgoing President George W. Bush and First Lady Laura Bush had left the White House. Earlier that morning, the Obamas had attended a service at

OPPOSITE: President Barack Obama delivers his inaugural address on Tuesday, January 20, 2009, at a ceremony staged on the West Front of the U.S. Capitol in Washington, D.C. ABOVE: President-elect Barack Obama, First Lady Laura Bush, President George W. Bush, and Michelle Obama at the White House on the morning of Inauguration Day.

St. John's Church, across Lafayette Park from the White House, then joined President and Mrs. Bush, Vice President–Elect Joe Biden and his wife, Jill, and congressional guests for coffee in the Blue Room. Shortly before 11 o'clock, the motorcades of President Bush and the president-elect and Mrs. Bush and Mrs. Obama departed for the inaugural ceremonies in front of the Capitol. We had approximately five hours to prepare a warm, welcoming home for the brand-new first family—to create magic in rooms that we hadn't even had a chance to see, much less measure. Which, looking back, seems truly impossible to achieve.

As the crowds swelled on the National Mall and the president-elect was sworn in, moving vans were positioned off the South Portico. One was carefully being loaded with the few remainders of the Bushes' personal effects, most of which had already been sent to their ranch or their new home in Dallas over the previous months (Laura Bush was meticulously organized), and the other trucks contained furniture we selected from the White House warehouse and the essentials the Obamas would need to start their new life—their books, clothes, some family photos, and things that were special to them. They were leaving their home in Chicago basically intact, so they could return periodically during the presidency. This was a major operation, as the movers could empty the trucks, but for security reasons only White House staff was permitted to move anything into the Residence. I think nearly everyone who works there, perhaps with the exception of the kitchen staff, is enlisted to assist on move-in day. It was great that several employees had previous transition experience, having served for one or both Bushes and the Clintons, and I was lucky to have my longtime collaborator Mark Matuszak and trusted design assistant Shannon Andrew come from my office to help me with this famously frenzied undertaking.

We tried our best to be super organized, but we were operating on minimal information. Weeks earlier, I had stumbled across an amazing website, whitehousemuseum.org, "the unofficial virtual museum of the president's residence," that provided photos, historical reference points, and color-coded floor plans. It proved to be invaluable. Not long after, Admiral Stephen Rochon, at that time the chief usher (essentially the COO of the White House), sent me a wonderful set of oversize portfolios referencing glossy color images of the individual rooms in the private quarters on the second and third floors, each numbered and keyed to a detailed floor plan. (I quickly learned that rooms were regularly referred to by those numbers—for instance, "220" was shorthand for the Family Sitting Room.) The photos depicted a range of rooms that had been decorated by the Bushes and their designer, Ken Blasingame, in an elegant, classic style. Though they had added several new

White House Residence First Floor

White House Residence Second Floor

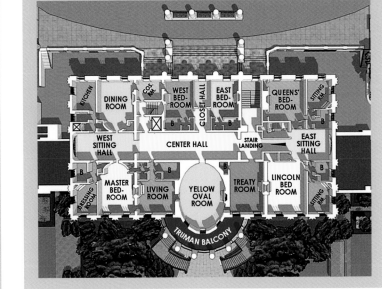

ABOVE: The extraordinary whitehousemuseum.org website features detailed floor plans, such as these, and both recent and historic photos, which proved invaluable to me; I continually referred to the site throughout the project. BELOW: Though my appointment as the Obamas' decorator wasn't officially announced until a few days before the January inauguration, their transition team connected me with the Bush White House staff in early December. I promptly received photos and detailed plans of the private floors of the Residence, which helped me visualize the rooms that were top priority; the first time I saw the interiors in person was move-in day.

First Family
Living Quarters

The White House
Third Floor

2008

Scale: 1/8" = 1'-0"

ABOVE: President and Mrs. Bush invited the president-elect and Mrs. Obama to the White House a few days following the November 4, 2008, election. After Laura Bush gave Michelle Obama the traditional tour of the private quarters in the Residence, they visited in the West Sitting Hall. LEFT: The following week, Jenna Bush Hager and Barbara Bush welcomed the Obama daughters for their own special tour. From left, Michelle Obama and her mother, Marian Shields Robinson, Sasha and Malia Obama, Jenna Bush Hager, and beloved White House butler James Ramsey.

ABOVE: Jenna, Barbara, and Laura Bush show Sasha and Malia that the ramp leading down from the Solarium to the Third Floor Corridor is perfect for sliding. RIGHT: The notes that Jenna and Barbara left for Sasha and Malia in their new bedrooms on Inauguration Day; it was a thoughtful gesture the Obama daughters would also extend when they left the White House eight years later. BELOW: Sasha tests out the seating in the Family Theater on the ground floor of the East Wing.

upholstered pieces, they also incorporated a great deal of furniture and lighting from the White House collection, so to our enormous relief most of the existing furnishings in the family quarters could remain as long as necessary.

President and Mrs. Bush had invited the president-elect and Mrs. Obama to the White House in November, just after the election, and in a thoughtful gesture Jenna and Barbara Bush gave Malia and Sasha their own special tour a week later. On Inauguration Day, they left welcoming notes for the girls to find in their new bedrooms, a kindness Malia and Sasha would also extend on their last day there. I tried in vain to schedule a scouting visit before the move-in, but it's traditionally not allowed. (I later read that incoming First Lady Jacqueline Kennedy urged Sister Parish, her famous New York decorator, to join her on her tour with outgoing First Lady Mamie Eisenhower. As decorators weren't permitted access until after the inauguration, Mrs. Kennedy tried to convince Mrs. Parish to pretend to be her secretary taking notes; not that surprisingly, she refused.)

In mid-December, about a month before the inauguration, the longtime White House curator William "Bill" Allman took me to the legendary White House support facility, which is in an undisclosed location just outside the city—the actual address is supposed to be confidential, so I literally never wanted to know where I was being driven. Mythically magical—it had been described to me as a treasure trove, a King Tut's tomb of wonderful stuff—in reality, it was somewhat disappointing, basically a repository for furnishings that the White House owns but that are not in use. I had visions of 18th-century French bergères, Monroe-era vermeil bibelots, and stacks of Gilbert Stuart portraits, but I soon realized that nearly everything of great quality or historic value is actually already inside the White House. However, Bill would become one of my best collaborators and allies in the coming years, my go-to guy for solving problems, and he now remains a very dear friend.

Though President and Mrs. Bush and Ken Blasingame had left the house in virtually pristine condition, making our jobs so much easier, January 20 was nevertheless a challenging, emotional, and harried day—for everyone involved. I remember that as I passed through the turnstile in the White House security booth that cold morning, I spotted a striking blonde brushing away tears as she maneuvered a small suitcase out the door, taking her personal things home on the last day of work. As it turns out, it was Amy Zantzinger, a social secretary for Mrs. Bush, and when we met some time later, we reminisced about that day. It was so impactful to realize that with this transfer of power on the global stage and its enormous waves of enthusiasm, there was also great emotion and sadness for those who were leaving a world

CLOCKWISE, FROM LEFT: I visited the fabled 40,000-square-foot White House support facility, located not far outside Washington, in mid-December and discovered rows of upholstered chairs, including reproductions of the gilded French armchairs purchased by President Monroe in 1817. The White House chief usher, Rear Admiral Stephen Rochon, helped me navigate the aisles of tiered steel racks; there was a massive selection to choose from, but I realized anything of great value was already in place at the White House. A mind-boggling array of chests, cabinets, and tables, all in various states of repair. A circa-1810 settee attributed to Duncan Phyfe and upholstered in a tailored silk stripe was a spare sofa for the Green Room, so it would not have been allowed for use in the family quarters. In addition to furniture, there were mirrors, paintings, and framed prints displayed on hanging racks; stacks of rolled carpets; and hundreds of lamps, vases, and bowls.

ABOVE: As soon as the presidential motorcades departed for the inauguration ceremony, moving vans positioned off the South Portico were sent into action: One truck was loaded with the last of the Bush family's personal effects as others delivered the Obamas' belongings, my selections from the warehouse, and art on loan from the National Gallery. BELOW: Barack Hussein Obama is sworn in as the 44th president of the U.S. by Chief Justice John Roberts as Michelle Obama holds a Bible used by Abraham Lincoln at his 1861 inauguration; a special platform was built for Sasha Obama to stand on. OPPOSITE: The monumental 2009 inaugural crowd was the largest in history, estimated at more than 1.8 million. For the first time, the full length of the National Mall—stretching from the Capitol to the Lincoln Memorial—was opened for public viewing of the ceremony.

CLOCKWISE, FROM ABOVE: We had only a few hours to prepare the family quarters while the inauguration and post-ceremony luncheon took place, and they were understandably chaotic. Though the housekeepers and White House staff were wonderful, we were installing rooms I'd decorated but never seen. I was confident the biggest impact would come from several pieces of large-scale contemporary art borrowed from the National Gallery, including Ed Ruscha's canvas *I Think I'll…*, which we hung over a sofa in the Center Hall. We displayed William H. Johnson's *Folk Scene – Man With Banjo* and *Lift Up Thy Voice and Sing*, paintings on plywood and paperboard, respectively, over a desk in the Third Floor Hall. *Source (Speculations)*, a screen print by Robert Rauschenberg, was installed over a console in the Center Hall, immediately to the right of the elevator vestibule. Carpets were steam-cleaned and vacuumed after the boxes were removed. In the midst of the move-in, packing boxes and clothes racks lined the West Sitting Hall.

after two full terms that felt like a virtual lifetime. That image has always stayed with me. It was not lost on me in that moment that in four or eight years, key Obama staff members would be going through that turnstile in the other direction as well.

Inside the Residence, the situation bordered on organized pandemonium. Unlike many presidential families, the Obamas had not packed up their family home, so for at least the first three months their private quarters were to be outfitted with a selection of pieces I had bought on their behalf, existing furnishings that the Bushes had used from the White House collection, and additional furniture and objects I chose from the warehouse. Mark, Shannon, and I were essentially decorating spaces on the run, so the move-in required a great deal of coordination—and there was also a hard stop. We had to be out by 3:30 P.M., when the president and first lady were expected back at the house before going to the viewing stand to watch the remainder of the parade. (In fact, we ended up having a bit more time when we received the distressing news that one of the president's earliest supporters, Senator Ted Kennedy, had collapsed at the inaugural luncheon and the family's return was delayed. Fortunately, the senator was released from the hospital the next day.)

When we planned the logistics of the move, I was informed by the Secret Service that due to security concerns over the unprecedented scale of the crowd expected at the inauguration, the area around the White House would be basically impermeable. I can't remember who thought it was a good idea that I come early—as in 2 or 3 A.M.—the night before the inauguration to sleep on a small cot in the shadowy, linoleum-floored basement. I actually considered this for a nanosecond before being stricken by the fear of the Secret Service cornering me in my pajamas if I took a wrong turn while searching for the bathroom. I declined the offer and won approval to sleep in my comfortable room at the Hay-Adams, just a short walk across the park. In fact, the move-in prep the day before the ceremony was so hectic and crazy that my partner, James, and I arrived at the Phillips Collection museum that evening, looking forward to a fundraising gala with a dinner cooked by famed chef Alice Waters, only to discover the museum shrouded in darkness. Much to our dismay, the event had taken place the night before, and the two of us ended up in our black tie waiting for a table at a local pub.

On the morning of Inauguration Day, with the help of the well-oiled housekeeping staff and my small team, I was working to make the private quarters feel like a family home within the allotted timeframe: making beds; placing books on shelves; fitting out bathrooms with new towels, soaps, and toothbrushes; spreading framed family photos around. It must have looked like a Marx Brothers movie on fast-forward—everyone was scurrying at warp

speed. The surreality of the situation was amplified by the fact that the White House itself is basically soundproof. Though I could see a flotilla of bouncing placards and balloons and sense the growing excitement as the moment of the swearing-in got closer, there was no roar of the crowd: I could hear virtually nothing outside the windows. My only sense of what was happening was gleaned from running downstairs to the Old Family Dining Room on the first floor, where a TV was somewhat haphazardly propped on a makeshift stand.

Late in the afternoon, I realized that because of the Obamas' delayed arrival, everyone else had finished preparing for the incoming first family and I was the only person left in the second-floor private quarters. Those stately rooms, so infused with centuries of history, were filled with a palpable sense of quiet anticipation. The last thing I did was place small bowls of water on the tables beside the president and first lady's bed, each floating a gardenia. I had the idea that after this most exciting of all days, with the realization of the extraordinary responsibilities they had just assumed, their sleep might be soothed by the scent of these flowers—perhaps the memory of what it was like to be in Hawaii, a place that they perceived as calm and restful, a place that they loved.

Then, my cell phone rang. Bizarrely, it was Barbara Walters, whom I'd known for several years. "Tell me something interesting about what's happening right now inside the Residence," she pleaded. "I'm about to go live." I don't recall what I said, but I knew, of course, that it had to be something completely innocuous; I remember that I wouldn't even tell her exactly where I was or what I was doing. I then headed downstairs, and moments later, in a remarkable, almost ludicrous synchronicity, I was watching Barbara on the TV repeat exactly what I had told her on the phone, just as I spotted the first family through the window, coming in from the cold to start their new life in their new home.

As I think back, even though I had previously only been in the downstairs public areas of the White House, I was able to piece together the physicality of the multitude of private spaces that I had not yet seen by studying floor plans and official photos, as well as the wealth of extraordinary vintage photos on the whitehousemuseum.org site, which offered a far wider range of angles. (That website would turn out to be everything to me for the next eight years.) The incredible scale of the White House rooms really hit home as soon as I walked in. Over the years, I've decorated some monumental houses for clients, but this was different. The verticality of the spaces was overwhelming—particularly on the second floor of the family quarters. The ceilings there are exceptionally tall for the proportion of the rooms, something that was not at all evident in the photos I had studied and was a bit of a shock. It became very apparent how important it would be to work with the ambient lighting, chandeliers, curtains, and large-scale art to bring the tall ceilings down to a more human scale and to dispel the shadows and dark areas created by the uneven illumination. I had tried to anticipate how the rooms would look when devoid of the warm, personal layers of the Bush family's furnishings, as I wanted to make the upstairs rooms very workable, more brightly lit, and completely filled with the color and life of this young family while respecting the grandeur of the environment.

OPPOSITE: I would periodically run downstairs from the family quarters to catch a few minutes of the ceremony and events on a TV perched in a corner of the Old Family Dining Room. ABOVE: From the window, we had a view of the president walking to the parade viewing stand on Pennsylvania Avenue.

The process of pulling together everything for that morning—all the preliminary decisions that needed to be made so that the house would be ready—was stressful but exciting. Many hands had been involved. Several people in my office had been focused on the project full-time for the previous six weeks, and Bill Allman (who had served at the White House for more than three decades) and his remarkable staff were instrumental in guiding us and helping us to understand the rules and restrictions—and how to best navigate through them. Also, before the inauguration, head housekeeper Jenny Botero proved to be invaluable as she managed to confirm measurements and specifications for us without disturbing President and Mrs. Bush. Mark Matuszak, who is an incredible artist, made stacks of extraordinary, highly detailed renderings and plans for each room, so we could show the Obamas what we envisioned the finished spaces would look like and, more important, feel like. Michelle Obama seemed very happy with our progress in just a few weeks and relieved when she saw that we were going to make the house as personal as possible as quickly as possible for her, the president, and their family.

The logistics were actually far more complicated than the multitude of aesthetic decisions we had to make. Though Congress appropriates $100,000 in federal funds to incoming presidents to help cover the cost of redecorating, most first families don't utilize the allocation. The Obamas were meticulous about paying for the decoration of the family quarters themselves, whereas the public rooms would be refurbished, when needed, through donations and funding from the White House Historical Association. We were very mindful that this would be a major investment for the family, and we shopped wisely and tried as much as possible to consolidate items and shipments to help keep costs driven by the scale of the project under control.

I had shipped some furniture I'd stockpiled in Los Angeles and also brought things that would make the space feel welcoming—a variety of pillows, some colorful lamps, cashmere throws, and a supply of spiced-orange scented candles. I had purchased an antique tiger-maple four-poster that I lent to the president and first lady as a temporary bed for the master bedroom, and we ordered mattresses and bed linens for it. We also found some fun,

OPPOSITE: The room in between the Master Bedroom and the Yellow Oval Room has served many roles in the past; the Bush family used it as a den, as would the Obamas. ABOVE: President and Mrs. Bush had decorated their family quarters in a subtle, elegant style, with many of the furnishings coming from the White House collection. We were relieved to be able to use the existing furniture and curtains in some of the rooms for at least the first few months, though I thought it was important for President and Mrs. Obama to sleep in a new bed their first night in office. I found a beautiful antique tiger-maple four-poster that would be perfect until we redecorated; *Nocturne*, the James McNeill Whistler painting that caught the president's eye, was hung to its left. RIGHT: I was pleased that the celadon neoclassical pattern chosen by the Bushes' designer, Ken Blasingame, for their Master Bedroom curtains, bed skirt, and wall covering created such a lovely, serene setting.

whimsical sheets and comforters for the girls, plus a group of inexpensive accessories from stores like Anthropologie to add color and wit to their bedrooms. We worked to create that extra layer you always need to make a home feel warm and inviting. With only five hours allotted for the move-in—and the White House family quarters comprise the top two stories of the six-floor building and measure about 20,000 square feet—we prioritized personalizing the primary rooms that they would use the most.

I was hopeful that the biggest and most immediate impact would be from several large-scale, colorful pieces of abstract art which were set for installation that first day. Not only would the bold works set the tone for our plans for the interiors, but they also helped me immediately make the private quarters feel more distinctive and expressive for this family. They were evocative of a fresh, new set of voices in the traditionally antiques-filled house and reflected the president and first lady's curiosity and interest in the worlds of culture and creativity.

Unfortunately, in my pursuit of art loans from various institutions across the country, I hit a couple of serious roadblocks early on. For example, I was obsessed with an amazing but massive Clyfford Still canvas in the collection of the National Gallery that would have required a cherry picker to get it through the front door while the inauguration was taking place. It was my one special request for the move-in, and though I relentlessly pushed the Secret Service and White House staff, I should not have been surprised when they said no. And I very much want-

ABOVE: After waving to the ebullient crowds that lined the one-and-a-half-mile parade route from the Capitol to the White House, the Obama family briefly stopped at the Residence before rejoining the parade at the presidential viewing stand constructed in front of the north façade of the building.

ed to borrow an iconic Wayne Thiebaud painting of delicious-looking cakes from the National Gallery to hang in the Center Hall near the girls' rooms. The museum informed me that it was perfect timing, as the painting had been headed to storage due to the renovation of the children's education area, but we had to cancel the loan when word leaked out that the Thiebaud might possibly be going to the White House. The press jumped to the wrong conclusion, calling to ask why we were taking such an important work off the wall and promoting the idea that we would be robbing schoolchildren of the chance to enjoy it at the museum. Nevertheless, I was able to secure other options, and despite my well-founded concerns about how the art-delivery truck would navigate the security checkpoints on Inauguration Day, it made it through and National Gallery curators Molly Donovan and Harry Cooper and their team were able to install powerful works by Robert Rauschenberg, Mark Rothko, Ed Ruscha, and Alma Thomas, among others. This was just the beginning of what would become an ongoing project to enrich and personalize those monumental spaces with impressive pieces of dramatic contemporary art.

Art always has been, and I imagine always will be, a very important part of the Obama world. (When they were first dating, the couple visited the Art Institute of Chicago, a museum with one of the most beautiful and rarified collections in America.) And the reward for the seemingly endless frustration of researching and obtaining art loans from museums—as well as my efforts to choose meaningful and historic pieces from the White House art collection with Bill Allman—came when President and Mrs. Obama invited an intimate group of about 50 friends, supporters, and staff back to the White House after the whirlwind excitement of all the inaugural balls. James and I were unbelievably honored to be asked. At one point, the president came up to me to say, with obvious delight, "There's a Whistler by my bed." (This was *Nocturne*, the James McNeill Whistler painting given to the White House during the Kennedy administration by diplomat-politician Averell Harriman and his wife, Marie.) I was thrilled that the president was pleased and that he was taken by the elegance and beauty of the work. Later, as we were leaving, he asked if I would come see him the next day to discuss the future renovation of his Oval Office. I shook my head in regret. "I can't," I told him. "We're heading back to L.A. in the morning." James was dumbfounded that I would say no to President Obama on his first night in the White House, the very first day of his new administration. In truth, I was completely exhausted by the days of preparation and the nonstop marathon of intensity and excitement; I wanted to go home to sleep, to recover and regroup, and to organize the next steps of the design process. I also needed to refocus attention on my other projects. And, as it turned out, the president put the redecoration of the Oval Office and areas of the West Wing on hold for well over a year in the face of his administration's concentration on the country's ongoing financial crisis. For at least the next day or two, my work was done.

4   DECORATOR-IN-CHIEF

After six weeks of planning for the Inauguration Day move—though an unbelievably brief period, it seemed like months, almost like dog years, as we had to get so much done—the Obama family was settling in with furniture we knew would easily get them through their first hundred days. That was when the real process of transformation began to pick up speed. Our focus was now on personalizing the family spaces, getting all of the soft furnishings— upholstery and curtains—finished, and having carpets installed, so the house would really become theirs and reflect their taste and style. I was intent on creating, as quickly as possible, a place that was warm and friendly, a place where they could retreat in privacy during the accelerated schedule that greets any new administration. Of paramount importance was making sure that it felt like a comfortable home to Malia and Sasha. Thankfully, Michelle Obama had convinced her mother, Marian Robinson, to move from Chicago to help care for the children, and we were preparing a suite of rooms for her on the third floor of the Residence.

The initial design schemes had started to take shape when I met with Mrs. Obama and her deputy chief of staff, Melissa Winter, soon after the family checked in to the Hay-Adams hotel at the beginning of January. The Hay-Adams is intimate and inviting, with charming interiors, and it turned out to be the perfect place for the family to acclimate to their new life in Washington. (I also stayed at the

Hay-Adams on all of my trips because of its proximity to the White House; located on the

OPPOSITE: Michelle Obama, a few weeks before the inauguration, at the family's suite at the Hay-Adams hotel in Washington, D.C. ABOVE: The president-elect, Mrs. Obama, and their daughters stayed on the top floor of the hotel, which offered a bird's-eye view of their new home.

other side of Lafayette Park, it's practically across the street. The staff there is lovely and discreet and always takes incredible care of me—plus, there's something particularly wonderful about being able to look out over the park and see the White House literally smack in front of you.) The Obamas had taken over the top floor for the two weeks before they moved to Blair House for the traditional pre-inaugural stay. Their suite offered a bird's-eye view not only of their future home, but also of a bright-blue banner stretched across a building just behind St. John's Church, which proclaimed WELCOME! MALIA AND SASHA.

At our first meeting in Washington, I remember hearing peals of laughter as soon as I got off the elevator on the Obamas' floor. Malia and Sasha were playing in the hall, running back and forth in front of the Secret Service agents who were stationed at every exit. I realized that I would soon be navigating an amazing juxtaposition, one in which formality and tradition would meet the unbridled enthusiasm of a young family. In that moment, I appreciated how special this family was, how the girls expressed such spirit and joy—even as their lives were being unimaginably transformed—and that the Obama family was deeply grounded, with a foundation that was both solid and strong.

It was crucial to start serious decision-making right at the outset. I had done a tremendous amount of research; I truly did my homework. Well before we had access to the White House, I was able to lay out photos and tear sheets of furniture and accessories and stacks of fabric and wallpaper samples that I had selected for the various rooms, as well as detailed renderings. My colleague Mark Matuszak created the most incredible renderings—

it's almost like we shared an unspoken language, like twins. I could describe what would be in the room and how it should appear, and he would make it come to life.

When the Obamas and I discussed what the family quarters should look and feel like, those design schemes became invaluable, as we updated them when changes were made. Mark had the idea of making a few red leather portfolios for the president and first lady, with covers stamped WHITE HOUSE DRAWINGS, to hold all of the sketches. We eventually kept them in a desk in the West Sitting Hall, and we would add each drawing, almost like a new chapter in a book, that they could refer to later. In the following months, after each room was put together or updated, I would often find the rendering of the space left on a chair or table in the room—it was clear that President Obama had compared it for accuracy. (Which at the time was rather daunting—and, honestly, somewhat nerve-racking.)

The White House staff's preparation for the new first family had also begun weeks before the Obamas arrived. Midafternoon on New Year's Eve, Bill Allman sent me an e-mail with photos of a variety of antique and contemporary rugs from the White House collection, ask-

OPPOSITE: A bright blue banner welcoming Malia and Sasha Obama stretched across the top of a building in view of the Hay-Adams. ABOVE: Collaborator Mark Matuszak created detailed renderings for the project from its inception, which the president and first lady then kept in special portfolios we made for them.

ing if we might want to use any in the family quarters, which ones should be cleaned, etc. We then wrote back and forth regarding the details and meticulous specifications—for instance, how much distance to allow from the edge of a rug to the wall. Bill and his team also started sending me photos of furniture options from the warehouse—an assortment of Chippendale chairs they thought might be suitable for the president's private dining room in the West Wing and nearly 20 different sofas for consideration for various rooms. It was a magpie mix from previous decors—including a pair of Betty Ford silk love seats and what I think might have been a Clinton-era nailhead-studded leather chesterfield, all in various states of repair. Also, the complex, very exciting, and behemoth process of researching and selecting art to display in the White House was well underway, with lists of options from the archives of various museums arriving daily.

As the Obama family adjusted to their new home, we made great progress, but the design process was still laborious at best. It's hard to believe, but in early 2009, there was no Wi-Fi at the White House and limited internet access for staff. At the time, the building's tech systems were reportedly managed by four separate agencies—including the president's Executive Office, the White House Communications Agency, the Secret Service, and the National Security Council—and upgrades had been sporadic and infrequent. Few White House staffers had individual email addresses, and many resorted to using their Gmail accounts. (This situation was one of the first things President Obama and his new team worked to resolve and progress was swift.) In the meantime, when I was not in Washington, Bill and his curatorial team and the staff of the chief usher, Admiral Rochon, needed to communicate with me constantly regarding specific room details and furnishings that were in storage, and they usually ended up sending photos and printed material through the mail or I paid for them to be FedExed. Now when I look back, this seems so archaic, and it truly was.

I made frequent trips to Washington, especially during the early stages of our work. Arriving the night before a meeting, I'd stay at the Hay-Adams, awake early, and get dressed in a suit—I tend to be more casual, but out of respect for the institution and the people who work within it, I always wore a suit at the White House. After walking across Lafayette Park with my canvas bag, which was usually weighted down with carefully organized samples and renderings, I would arrive at the security outpost for the East Gate. As you would imagine,

OPPOSITE, FROM TOP: While Barack Obama was being sworn in at the Capitol, White House staff prepared the Oval Office for the new president. Names and extensions on the phone were updated, a few new pieces of art were installed, and a signature bowl of apples was placed on the coffee table. The morning following ten inaugural balls and an after-party for friends and family, President Obama enters the Oval Office from the West Colonnade for the first full day of his administration; at far left is his personal aide, Reggie Love.

there are multiple layers of security at the White House, and more often than not, I would get stuck at the very first one. You hand your driver's license to a Secret Service agent through the bars of the first gate, and they check the visitor log. Though Bill Allman would always have placed me on the list, there would be some snafu and I would invariably be told that my name was missing and wait, shivering in the snow or sweating from the heat and humidity, until a call was made and I was allowed up to the next checkpoint and then to walk through the X-ray machines. This literally went on for years, even though the guards and I came to know one another and they were super nice. It's simply protocol; rules are rules at the White House.

Bill would greet me after I made it through the gauntlet, and we would go to his office on the ground floor until it was time to meet with the first lady. The meetings were always incredibly efficient, very productive. I would go with very strong ideas, and it was such a pleasure to try to work them out—in truth, it was a pleasure even just to be in those fascinating histor-

ic rooms. Each visit was important to me, and I always kept top of mind something that Casey Ribicoff, who was a very dear, longtime friend, told me. Casey was the elegant widow of Senator Abe Ribicoff, a three-term senator from Connecticut and former governor, who had previously served in President Kennedy's cabinet. The senator and Casey had been regular guests at the White House, and she was enormously helpful to me when I took on this project, sharing advice on how to best navigate life in Washington. In her smoky, worldly voice, she said, "You'll see, no matter how often you visit the White House, you'll never get blasé. It's always special, and your heart will swell with a sense of patriotism every single time." And, as in everything, Casey was always right.

One of the first official things I was asked to do was to consult on a few remaining elements of the refurbishment project begun by the Bush administration that were still in process. New carpets were needed for the Ground Floor Corridor, which is vast—it's about 161 feet

OPPOSITE, FROM TOP: When I returned to Washington a week after the inauguration, it was a priority to find the president a comfortable desk chair, as President Bush's black leather chair (*far right*) was being shipped to Texas. President Obama's days were so tightly scheduled that it was well into the evening before he could try various options to replace it. Michelle Obama and her deputy chief of staff, Melissa Winter, offered their opinions from the sofa. It turned out that this chair, which I pulled from my storage in L.A., was perfect, and I simply loaned it to the president until we updated his office the following year. ABOVE: The security outpost at the East Gate was the first of a few checkpoints I had to pass through each time I visited the White House.

long and 17 feet wide. The wool had already been dyed a specific red, but the rug design wasn't yet confirmed. I wanted to be as respectful as possible of Laura Bush and her interior designer, Ken Blasingame, as we completed what they had initiated. We proposed a new star motif, and a discussion ensued—how big should the stars be, and what color? How far apart should they be placed? And then, after more discussion, we reinstated the long-standing design of solid red with a gold egg-and-dart border, though we tweaked the border detail a bit. The carpets were finally installed a year later, in the spring of 2010, and Bill sounded distinctly relieved when he emailed me that the first lady had loved them.

Just as with the Bushes, near the end of President Obama's second term, we also had a few restoration projects underway that we were able to hand off to the incoming administration to complete. President and Mrs. Bush and their teams had been incredibly generous during our transition, and they set a remarkable example for us. In fact, the ground floor project we inherited from them taught me a critical lesson early on: A hall carpet should be a nonpartisan issue. The legacy of the White House and the tradition of its design reflects a generosity of spirit that should always take precedence over the sometimes divisive culture of American politics. This was enormously important to Michelle and Barack Obama—and to all of us who worked to help bring their ideas, plans, and commitments to fruition.

Throughout the eight years I worked on the White House, there were many obstacles to overcome and much bureaucracy and red tape to contend with, but the Obamas were always more than gracious, thoughtful, and highly appreciative. Bill Allman was hugely instrumental in helping us get the family settled promptly so we could embark on the next design phase. He wore so many hats: Not only was he in the rarefied position of being the acknowledged expert on the history of the White House decorative-arts collection and architecture (he had been on staff since the Carter administration and could speak with authority about the historic importance and technical aspects of regilding the 19th-century Monroe chairs), but he was also adept at removing holiday-party red-wine stains from carpets and reorganizing rooms for a child's birthday celebration. The ideal steward and caretaker of the legacy of the White House, Bill knew its ins and outs and had a wonderful feel for it as both a structure and an iconic and historic ideal.

Bill is an expert on the multitude of White House collections, including antique furniture, porcelain, and silver, and especially its wide and diverse group of art. He was a quick study in terms of all the various contemporary works that the Obamas and I wanted to bring in, so much so that he became the face of the introduction of contemporary art in the

CLOCKWISE, FROM TOP: President Obama walks down the Ground Floor Corridor following a holiday reception; one of my early assignments was to update the carpets for the vast space. Mark Matuszak's rendering for the project. White House curator William "Bill" Allman sent me photos of the carpet samples in process.

MICHAEL S SMITH INTERIORS
ILLUSTRATION / MARK MATUSZAK

CENTER HALL PERSPECTIVE
1600 PENNSYLVANIA AVENUE
WASHINGTON, DC

MARCH 4, 2009

White House to the press, handling nearly all matters regarding the selection and display of this new art. Acutely aware that everything we did was part of a historic continuity, he was constantly vigilant that we respect the past and, if possible, try to replicate or reference it when we could. He was discreet, protective, and especially mindful that moving a piece of furniture was both potentially risky to that piece as well as a moment in the history of the building, so everything we did was meticulously photographed and documented.

Bill's number one concern was to not ever be intrusive to the normal pace of the first family's life. Having worked in the White House throughout many administrations, he understood the importance of the small amount of private downtime the Obama family would have. The president and first lady were unfailingly patient, so Bill was perhaps even more protective of the impact of any intervention in the private quarters. It was paramount that no one interrupt their personal time, and he wanted them to feel as if they lived in a normal house, without people coming and going constantly. Any work to hang a painting, move furniture, or do a repair was scheduled when the family was out, and the more complicated design projects were always done while the Obamas were away on their two annual vacations. Bill wanted no disruption or ripples in the pond of their private life.

So, in addition to our awareness of the budget constraints, we were also forced to be super organized about every aspect of the project and to present as much material as possible at

ABOVE: Bill Allman in the Green Room of the White House. OPPOSITE: Replacing worn sofa fabric in the Vermeil Room was one of the projects I worked on with the Committee for the Preservation of the White House.

each meeting, usually schemes for entire rooms, so we could make the most efficient use of our limited time. We met on an as-needed basis with Mrs. Obama and were always hyper-aware that her schedule was packed and what little free time she did have she wanted to spend with her daughters and husband. She has such enthusiasm and curiosity, and she always made me feel like the meetings were a fun break for her during the balance of her more official duties during the day.

Bill also ensured that we understood the myriad regulations required by a host of govern-ment entities—the General Services Administration, the National Park Service, etc.—and that we conformed to traditional guidelines set by previous administrations. For example, every-thing that we ordered for the family quarters—from floor lamps to coffee tables to down duvets—had to be inspected by the Secret Service in an off-site warehouse before it could be delivered to the White House. This always added a certain time delay to when things could be put in place in the private quarters. As gracious and as helpful as the warehouse staff and White House team were, there was no opportunity whatsoever for the usual last-minute FedEx of pillows or lamps. And the overall designs and individual pieces that we ultimately proposed for the public rooms would not only be run by Bill for his collaborative opinions, both historic and aesthetic, but would also be reviewed by the members of the Committee for the Preservation of the White House, several of whom were newly appointed by President Obama. The committee, formed as part of Jackie Kennedy's vision to restore the White House as a "living museum," was first known as the Fine Arts Committee. In 1964, it was officially renamed and sanctioned by the Johnson administration to advise the president and first lady

and the director of the National Park Service regarding the protection of the historic aspect of the White House public spaces. Working in tandem with Bill and his curatorial team, as well as the White House Historical Association (WHHA)—which oversees the endowment and acquisition trusts—the committee reviews refurbishing projects and the funding of additions to the White House collection of furnishings and fine art. By tradition, the White House decorator is also usually named to this group, and I was thrilled and honored to be asked to join.

I always looked forward to our meetings, as well as the dialogues they produced. Honestly, I was relieved that there were so few things that received any kind of pushback and remember only a handful of instances when any of the committee members and I were not in total agreement. For example, late in the second term, the group wasn't keen on a fabric I had selected to re-cover two sofas in the Vermeil Room (one is prominently placed under the celebrated Aaron Shikler portrait of Mrs. Kennedy). The damask sofa upholstery was more than a decade old and beginning to wear thin. The committee members decided that the embossed mohair velvet I had found was perfect, they simply preferred a different color. Bill e-mailed photos of the swatches all around, and a deep-green version that matched the curtains replaced the wine-colored option that coordinated with the rug. And that was perhaps the biggest challenge we had to contend with.

We were a relatively diverse group, some with connections to the first family, but all with relevant backgrounds and a deep knowledge of American decorative-arts history. We were excited to gather together in meetings at the White House or via communications meticulously organized by Bill to work on a project that was so impressive and inspiring. We understood the gravitas of our mission—and the impact that everything we selected and every decision we made would become part of the legacy of this presidency.

I had to constantly balance on the fine line between the desire to have the White House reflect the Obamas' point of view and keeping my eye on the vast history of the building itself. It was essential that I be respectful not only of its illustrious past, but also of its complex roles as a museum, the office of the president, and his family residence. Every option and decision had to be considered from every angle, and contributors needed to be vetted to ensure they were above reproach. We would all be part of this highly visible and historic chapter in the very long history of America's most iconic building. There was truly no margin for error.

OPPOSITE, FROM TOP: My Committee for the Preservation of the White House appointment was signed in 2010 by Barack Obama and then–Secretary of State Hillary Clinton. The first lady with members of the committee in 2016. Seated from left, chief usher Angella Reid, Leslie Bowman, Thelma Golden, curator William Allman, myself, Linda Johnson Rice, and chairman Jonathan Jarvis; standing from left, Richard Nylander, John Frank, Dr. Anita Blanchard, Lonnie Bunch, Michelle Obama, Rusty Powell, Laura Paulson, John Stanwich, and Wendy Cooper.

Barack Obama
President of the United States of America,

To all who shall see these presents, Greeting:

Know Ye, that reposing special trust and confidence in the *Integrity and Ability* _____ of _____ *Michael S. Smith, of California,* _____ I do appoint *him* _____ *a Member of the Committee for the Preservation of the White House,* _____ and do authorize and empower *him* to execute and fulfil the duties of that Office according to law, and to have and to hold the said Office, with all the *powers and privileges* _____ thereunto of right appertaining, unto *him* the said _____ *Michael S. Smith,* _____ *during the pleasure* of the President of the United States for the time being. _____

In testimony whereof, I have caused these Letters to be made Patent, and the Seal of the United States to be hereunto affixed.

Done at the City of Washington this _____ *third* _____ day of _____ *March,* _____ in the year of our Lord two thousand *ten* _____ and of the Independence of the United States of America, the two hundred and *thirty-fourth* _____

By the President:

Hillary Rodham Clinton

Secretary of State.

5   UPSTAIRS AT THE WHITE HOUSE

As exhilarating as it was to work in the White House—even the thought of designing the Oval Office for this history-making president was somewhat mind-blowing—the most important aspect of the project was to create a home in which Michelle and Barack Obama's young family would be able to thrive. The delineation between their private and public lives was especially critical because their daughters were so small, and it was my responsibility to help them feel at ease and have a sense of privacy in this iconic building. As Melissa Winter, the first lady's deputy chief of staff, told me, "I think it was very important to Mrs. Obama that upstairs would be a place where the girls could come home from school and really feel like, 'This is where we live.'"

The president-elect and first lady had copies of my design books, and when asked to flag photos they liked, the rooms they were drawn to were perhaps more traditional and formal than the interiors of their Chicago home yet shared its elegance and warmth. I had the sense that they had faith I could work within the architecture of the Residence and create rooms that were as inviting and comfortable as the private quarters of President and Mrs. Bush but more in sync with their personal lifestyle. I think that's one of the reasons I was hired, in addition to being super straightforward about timing and budget. I have always been fiercely loyal to them, and they trusted me; I also like to think I made the process fun.

The space itself is daunting—the family quarters comprise the top two floors of the 55,000-square-foot, six-story Residence (there are two basements and a ground floor; the third floor is attic level). The second floor features a center hall plus 16 rooms and six and a half bathrooms, and there is a wide corridor and 20 rooms with nine bathrooms on the third floor. There are semiprivate rooms, such as the Lincoln and Queens' bedrooms

OPPOSITE: A 2013 meeting on the go with First Lady Michelle Obama and members of her staff as we walked through the East Colonnade, which overlooks the Jacqueline Kennedy Garden.

and sitting rooms; the Treaty Room, where the president would meet with his staff; and the Yellow Oval Room, where the Obamas entertained guests. There were rooms I barely touched, and others that required continual tweaks over the eight years they were in office.

Though the Obamas selected furniture, lamps, and rugs from the White House collection, they purchased the majority of their new furnishings. Mrs. Obama wrote in her memoir, *Becoming*, that they were vigilant about this, using saved royalties from the president's two best-selling books. Upkeep and maintenance projects, as well as renovations such as the installation of ceiling lighting in some gloomy rooms on the second floor, were funded by the WHHA. And in the patriotic tradition of some of my predecessors, I donated my services to the White House. Because there was so much red tape involved in the project, I sometimes found it easier to simply loan the Obamas furniture or objects to streamline the decorating process, and as the Yellow Oval Room best exemplified the grace and elegance of the Residence, I formally donated a set of chairs and an Oushak rug that were beautifully suited to it.

As you can imagine, many vendors wanted to showcase their work in the White House, and when I arrived in Washington, I was handed files of correspondence from people offering to donate everything from furniture and fine art to Bill Allman's and my personal favorite, a painting in the style of Yves Klein done by a lady's cat. There are quite stringent rules about what could be accepted, and more than a few donations that would have been useful in the project were rejected because the giver didn't pass the vetting process. When I was being vetted, I received a bone-chilling voicemail about "investigating something problematic in your record" that sounded like I had robbed a bank. It turned out to be a couple of traffic tickets, but the security agent remained remarkably scornful.

Extremely conscious of the costs of outfitting these substantial spaces, I was very mindful of the impact of my design recommendations. Fortunately some vendors offered professional discounts, while others, inspired by the Obamas, generously donated furnishings to the White House holdings. I also thought it was important to be cost-effective and relatable by adding great finds at affordable prices — including colorful ikat pillows from Crate & Barrel, playroom furniture from Walmart, and Pottery Barn's chic candleholders.

Always top of mind was the mission that Mrs. Obama and I shared of focusing on makers and artisans from across the country. For instance, when I discovered the only china in the family kitchen was formal White House porcelain, I ordered them classic Bennington Potters stoneware from Vermont, a daily reminder for the Obamas and their children of the beauty and craftsmanship of an iconic design made in America.

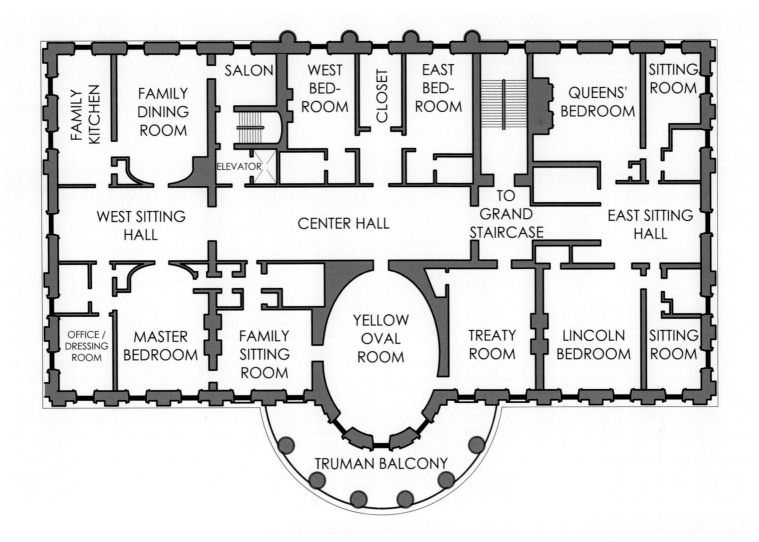

ABOVE: The floor plan for the family quarters on the second floor of the Residence, which includes private rooms as well as spaces that have a more official role, such as the Yellow Oval Room, the Treaty Room, and the Lincoln and Queens' bedrooms. RIGHT: In the China Room, located on the Ground Floor, I discuss a selection of chairs with (*from left*) Michelle Obama, deputy chief of staff Melissa Winter, social secretary Jeremy Bernard, and curator Bill Allman. The antique lyre-back chair in the center is from a suite I donated to the White House collection to be used in the Yellow Oval Room.

MASTER BEDROOM

Though Michelle Obama made it clear from the outset that her daughters' rooms and the third-floor suite where Mrs. Robinson would live were our number one decorating focus, it was personally very important to me to design a master bedroom that would be a true refuge for the president and first lady. It was integral to my entire narrative of them moving into this historic building that we create a romantic, private space for them to be alone as a couple. It was essential that their bedroom be elegant and serene. I covered the Master Bedroom walls in an oatmeal-colored Chinese paper by Gracie that we used as a background, adding a soft wash of paint. There was an interesting historical aspect to this for me, as Gracie had made the incredibly beautiful paper, hand-painted with birds in flight, that Nancy Reagan installed in the space decades earlier. I thought it was appropriate that the Obamas have this more modern interpretation of the same idea. I was always thinking about linking with tradition but making everything very much of our time and more relevant to the taste and mindset of this special family.

I commissioned a carpet to be handmade by Mitchell Denburg in a pale celadon, and we re-covered the existing Bush-era armchairs in a blue-green Manuel Canovas cotton blend and the sofa in a straw-colored woven pattern from my Jasper fabric collection. The mirrored coffee table was inspired by a design by Samuel Marx, a midcentury Chicago architect and designer; I liked the subtle nod to their hometown. We chose an early-19th-century American mahogany bed from the White House collection, which was easily adapted to king size. I had proposed a canopy bed to them early on, and though the president wasn't keen on the idea

OPPOSITE: Located on the second floor of the Residence's family quarters, the tall windows of the Master Bedroom offer a sunny view of leafy trees and the wide South Lawn below. The cotton sateen bed linens are by Nancy Koltes, and the matelassé coverlet is from RH.

The image shows fabric and textile swatches with labels reading "MANUEL CANOVAS", "4333-40 FREGOLI", "SAMUEL & SONS", and "COWTAN & TOUT".

at first, he graciously deferred to his wife, saying, "If Michelle wants it, then we can have it." It's ironic, but nearly everyone who is initially hesitant when I suggest a canopy bed ends up loving it. I find it creates a real sanctuary in a room, a retreat within a retreat—and it can be especially helpful in establishing a sense of architecture within a minimalist space.

I have always been highly focused on making beds as comfortable as possible—it's an enormous priority for me. I care about luxuriously smooth sheets, the softness of the pillows and weight of the duvet, the texture of a blanket. What makes a bed really wonderful

ABOVE: The Master Bedroom's muted color palette features soft blues and warm neutrals. I conceived of it as a soothing, serene space—a true refuge. OPPOSITE: An early rendering by Mark Matuszak.

for my clients isn't just how it looks, but how it actually feels. A great mattress is essential, and I think a down mattress cover gives the best foundation. I ordered a few sets of classic cotton sateen sheets by Nancy Koltes, as I prefer linens with a satin finish and a light sheen to them; they feel so cool when you slide into bed. We used a raw silk by Larsen for the canopy, curtains, and bed skirt and installed swing-arm lamps tucked within the bed curtains — they're so practical for reading. Instead of nightstands, generous antique side tables flanked the bed, as did a pair of antiqued mercury-glass mirrors from my Jasper line. The mercury glass gave a softly diffused reflection of the sun-splashed space.

President Obama asked us to move the Whistler painting from beside the window on his side of the bed to over the mantel for a better view (they didn't really use the fireplace in that room), and I loaned them a distinctive oval canvas by the surrealist Augustus Vincent Tack, which was hung nearby, as were two Giorgio Morandi still lifes borrowed from the National Gallery of Art. The Morandis encapsulated everything I wanted for this room — the shapes were simple and pure, and the tones were muted. They were exquisite, distilled compositions that perfectly reflected the bedroom's soothing, almost matte palette.

MICHAEL S SMITH INTERIORS
ILLUSTRATION / MARK MATUSZAK

MASTER BEDROOM
1600 PENNSYLVANIA AVENUE
WASHINGTON, DC

JANUARY 12, 2009

PREVIOUS PAGES: The desk-and-bookcase is late 18th century, and the high-post bed is early 19th century; both are American. The bed's canopy, curtains, and bed skirt are of a Larsen raw silk. The embroidered pillow in the foreground is by Jed Johnson Home, and the wallpaper is by Gracie; the rug was custom made by Mitchell Denburg. ABOVE: Still lifes by Giorgio Morandi from the National Gallery of Art and a circa-1903 A. H. Davenport & Co. armchair. RIGHT: Augustus Vincent Tack's *Abstraction* is displayed to the left of the marble mantel while *Nocturne*, by James McNeill Whistler, hangs above it; the Samuel Marx–inspired coffee table is by Jasper Furniture.

FIRST LADY'S DRESSING ROOM / OFFICE AND SALON

Laura Bush's subtle, elegant hand was so evident in the First Lady's Dressing Room and Private Office, which was adjacent to the Master Bedroom, that all we added were a comfortable armchair and ottoman and some framed photos. Michelle Obama has said that she was reminded that she was part of a "humble continuum" when Mrs. Bush pointed out the view of the Rose Garden and Oval Office through the window beside the desk, saying that it gave her comfort to know that President Bush was working not far away. Mrs. Bush explained that First Lady Hillary Clinton had shown her the view, as First Lady Barbara Bush had also pointed it out to Mrs. Clinton on her first visit.

Though FLOTUS maintained an official office in the East Wing, this was her office at home, the place where she would read the daily briefing binders delivered to her and the president every evening during dinner with their daughters. She would spend a few hours each night reviewing staff memos regarding her many initiatives and drafts for event remarks and speeches. The nearby Salon—where we displayed personal photos and the celebrated cover of *The New Yorker* featuring the family dog Bo—also did double duty as an office, with a built-in desk for staff to brief the first lady as she was prepped for events. In fact, Melissa Winter, her deputy chief of staff, told me the Salon was the upstairs space that served almost like an air lock between Mrs. Obama's public and private lives. If she ever needed to speak with the first lady about an important matter during off-hours, she would text her and request a quick meeting there, never wanting to disturb the family in their home.

MICHAEL S SMITH INTERIORS
ILLUSTRATION / MARK MATUSZAK
FIRST LADY'S DRESSING ROOM
1600 PENNSYLVANIA AVENUE
WASHINGTON, DC
FEBRUARY 6, 2010

OPPOSITE: The First Lady's Dressing Room and Private Office was adjacent to the Master Bedroom, with views south and west. ABOVE: Our initial rendering of the space.

ABOVE: Michelle Obama's private office was warm, cozy, and inviting. OPPOSITE: A wall of framed photos and Bo Obama's celebrated cover of *The New Yorker* added warmth and personality to the Salon.

MALIA AND SASHA OBAMA'S BEDROOMS

The Obamas' daughters' rooms were my first order of business, as FLOTUS wanted to ensure her young girls felt comfortable in this exciting but very unfamiliar new space. Our guiding principle was for their spaces to be fun and colorful, with a whimsical nod to the historic. We started by installing wallpapers handmade by Elizabeth Dow, an artist turned wallpaper and textile designer, in both rooms. Wide candy-pink stripes were selected for Sasha, and a classic American crosshatch pattern in robin's-egg blue for Malia's room.

We decided on a Swedish-style bed for Malia, which was designed by Suzanne Kasler and upholstered in an amethyst ikat stripe, and the desk, tables, and chair were painted in cheerful pops of color. I had a faux-bamboo bed from my Jasper line of furniture made for Sasha and enameled her bureau, nightstands, and armchair in an equally bright palette. We wanted the spaces to be feminine and fun, with beanbag chairs, comfortable sofas, and vivid hues and patterns. But I thought it was also important for the rooms to reflect a sense of history, as they feature remarkable architectural detail—there are beautiful moldings, classic fireplace mantels, and arched bookcases. We decided to paint the bookcase niches in striking colors that would look fresh and vibrant to contrast with and highlight the bright white millwork.

We made a folding screen for each room, covered with wallpaper by Adelphi Paper Hangings in historic American patterns printed in unexpected colors. They became a fun focal point in the bedrooms and helped to visually step down the scale of the soaring spaces. On Inauguration Day, we hung two Robert Rauschenberg lithographs in Malia's room and Sasha had a painting by Jacob Lawrence, which happily coexisted with the girls' signed Hannah Montana posters propped against their mantels. Not long after, their floors were covered with overscale organic-motif carpets custom made by Anthropologie—Malia and Sasha were literally surrounded by lighthearted, artful pattern and a rainbow of colors.

But there was even more. It was through my friend Keith Johnson, the former creative director and buyer-at-large at Anthropologie, that I found what would be the most interesting aspect of

OPPOSITE: From left, William H. Johnson's *Booker T. Washington Legend* and *Children Dance*, on loan from the Smithsonian American Art Museum, were displayed in Malia's room against walls clad in an Elizabeth Dow paper. The bed, by Suzanne Kasler for Hickory Chair, was upholstered in a Peter Dunham Textiles ikat stripe; the side tables are by Mitchell Gold and Bob Williams; and the rug was custom made by Anthropologie. The chandelier is a one-of-a-kind design produced by the Magpie Art Collective, a South African craft studio.

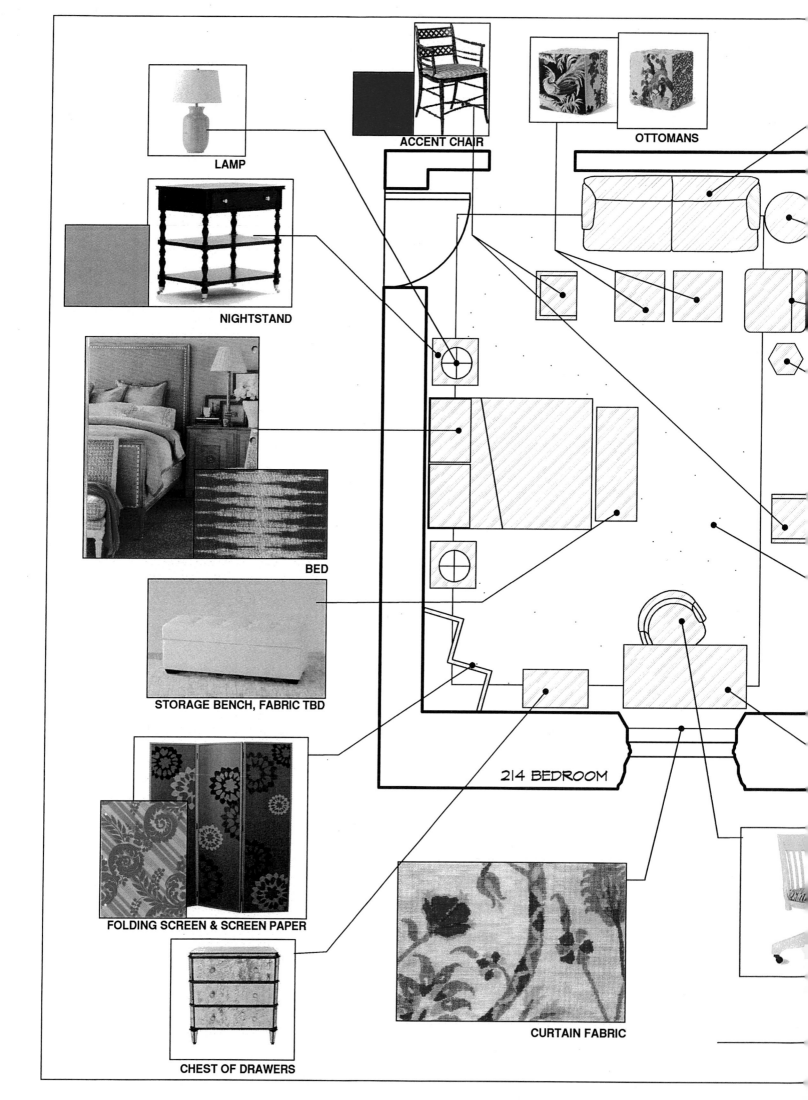

LAMP

ACCENT CHAIR

OTTOMANS

NIGHTSTAND

BED

STORAGE BENCH, FABRIC TBD

214 BEDROOM

FOLDING SCREEN & SCREEN PAPER

CURTAIN FABRIC

CHEST OF DRAWERS

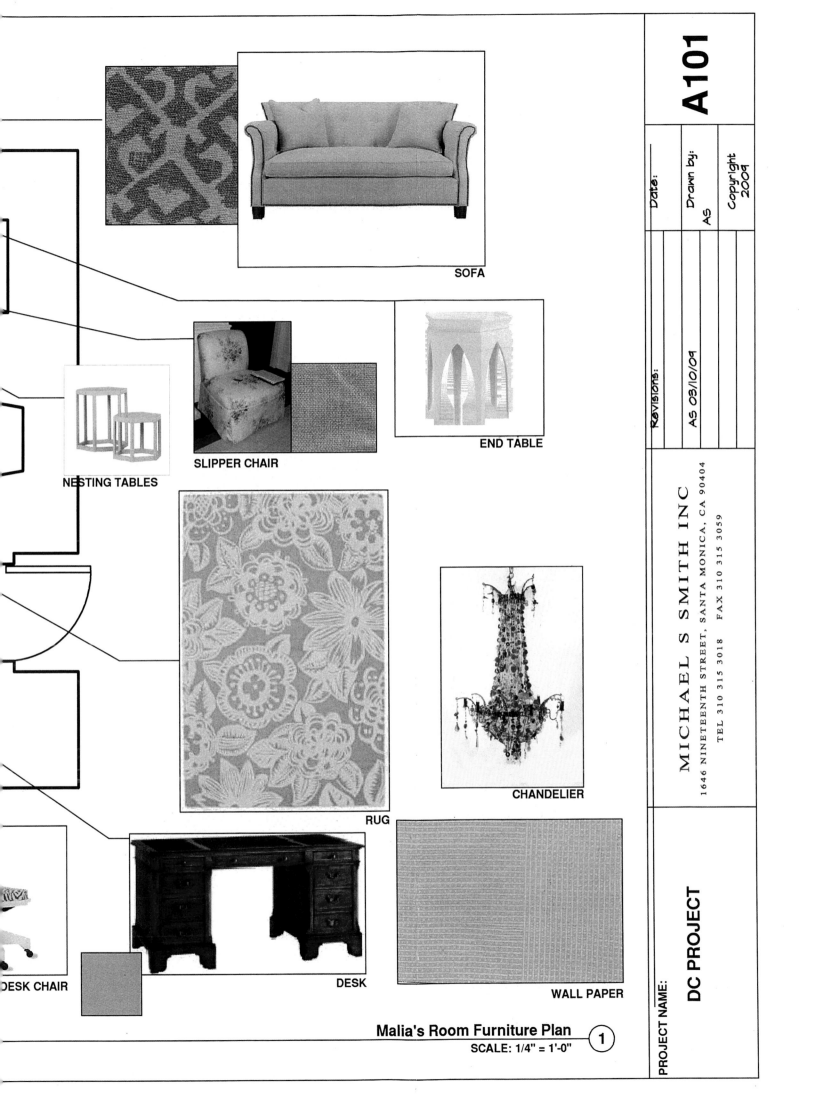

SOFA

SLIPPER CHAIR

NESTING TABLES

END TABLE

RUG

CHANDELIER

DESK CHAIR

DESK

WALL PAPER

Malia's Room Furniture Plan
SCALE: 1/4" = 1'-0"
(1)

MICHAEL S SMITH INC
1646 NINETEENTH STREET, SANTA MONICA, CA 90404
TEL 310 315 3018   FAX 310 315 3059

Date:

Drawn by:

AS

Copyright
2009

Revisions:

AS 03/10/09

A101

PROJECT NAME:

DC PROJECT

the two rooms, the element that tied the entire narrative together. Keith had discovered an artisanal group called the Magpie Art Collective in South Africa and used their pieces with great success in his stores, inspiring me to commission special ceiling fixtures for the girls' rooms. Based on traditional chandeliers, they were covered with trinkets, bottle caps, and pieces of plastic—found objects fashioned into something really wonderful and in keeping with the iconic 18th-century lighting forms used in the White House, but with a whimsical new twist.

One day, after the girls had settled in, I received a call from FLOTUS's office asking if I could quickly get alarm clocks for their rooms. Apparently, after living at the Hay-Adams hotel for a few weeks, they had cleverly figured out how to request morning wake-up calls from the White House operator. Although I found their ingenuity disarming, their mother appropriately felt the calls might be a distraction for the staff. Michelle Obama was always very clear with me and the family-quarters staff that this was a temporary home—either four or eight years—and that though she was very appreciative of the kindness and care that was shown to them, her daughters needed to know how to function normally in the real world. Both she and Mrs. Robinson made sure Malia and Sasha were responsible for things that most children are, like learning to do their own laundry and make their beds. However, I will always have a soft spot for Sasha and her incredibly savvy, pragmatic view—she slept in just half of her bed after realizing it would then take half as long to make it in the morning. And she was only seven years old.

PREVIOUS PAGES: I would present renderings, swatches, product tear sheets, and detailed design schemes to enable Michelle Obama to better visualize each room. ABOVE: Malia's palette included blues and purples and a pop of terracotta, with a Peter Dunham Textiles ikat and floral and geometric fabrics by Carolina Irving Textiles.

CLOCKWISE, FROM TOP LEFT: We painted the bookcase niche a sunny yellow to contrast with the subtle blue walls and bright white millwork, a reflection of Mrs. Obama's wish to see pops of color in the rooms. Sasha's color palette featured pinks and greens, along with lyrical prints by Raoul Textiles. We enameled this English Regency–style armchair from the Historic Charleston Collection a bright Benjamin Moore blue for Sasha. The tall ladders used for the curtain installation give an idea of the enormous verticality of the rooms on the second floor. The bathrooms had been redone during the previous administration and I loved them—they were big spaces in floor-to-ceiling white with white marble–tiled baths. We simply added flowery shower curtains, bath rugs, and towels to make them more cheerful. Elizabeth Dow made the pink striped wallpaper for Sasha and a blue crosshatch for Malia's room. Swing-arm lamps from Circa Lighting were installed next to both Sasha's and Malia's beds. FOLLOWING PAGES: I worked with Sasha over the years to adapt her bedroom from that of a seven-year-old little girl to one suited to a smart, style-conscious teenager.

FAMILY DINING ROOM

The Family Dining Room—located in the northwest corner of the second floor, just across the West Sitting Hall from the Master Bedroom—has a storied past. Originally designed as a storeroom and then reconfigured as a bedchamber, for a time the space was called the Prince of Wales Room after an 1860 visit by Edward Albert, then the Prince of Wales, to President James Buchanan; a few presidents have even used it as their master bedroom. Mary Todd Lincoln placed the elaborate Lincoln bed there, and it's reportedly where 11-year-old Willie Lincoln died of typhoid fever in 1862. Nearly a century later, in 1949, the space held Margaret Truman's infamous piano that almost crashed through the ceiling of the room below, prompting the radical four-year reconstruction of the Residence. And in 1961, when confronted with the needs of her young family, Jacqueline Kennedy and her decorator Sister Parish revamped the suite to serve as a family dining room by installing an adjacent working kitchen. This key renovation transformed the upstairs quarters into a self-contained private apartment for the first time in the history of the Residence. (Previous first families took most of their meals on the State Floor, in the room which is now known as the Old Family Dining Room.)

During their early-1960s restoration project, the Kennedys had installed a historic Zuber paper with Revolutionary War scenes on the dining room walls, a gift funded by famed New York philanthropist Brooke Astor. In 1974, when Betty Ford moved in, she found the scenics unsettling and asked to remove the paper in favor of walls painted a sunny yellow. Rosalynn and Jimmy Carter restored the antique paper, and it remained in place through the terms of Ronald Reagan and George H. W. Bush. When Hillary and Bill Clinton arrived in 1993, their decorator, Kaki Hockersmith, installed a pale-green silk wall covering on top of the paper, which Laura and George Bush eventually updated with a champagne-colored damask.

OPPOSITE: FLOTUS's focus on making the Residence more relevant by mixing contemporary art with historic antiques is reflected here; importantly, she also offered the always-tuxedoed butler staff a more casual uniform option when public events weren't scheduled. Josef Albers's paintings *Homage to the Square: Midday* and *Homage to the Square: Elected II* are displayed above an antique mahogany sideboard; the sculpture is *The Bow*, by Edgar Degas. The paintings and sculpture were on loan from the Hirshhorn Museum and Sculpture Garden.

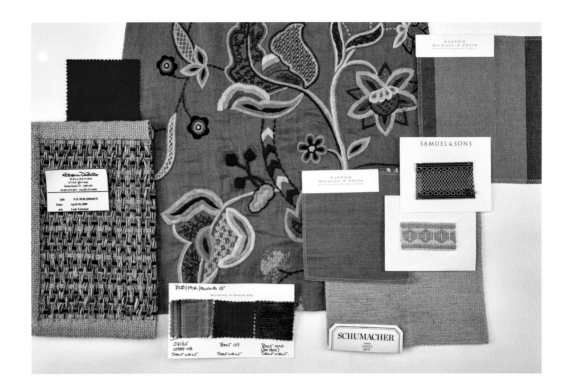

When I began to rethink the Family Dining Room for the Obamas, I was thrilled to learn that we could remove the existing wall fabric to reveal Mrs. Kennedy's French paper beneath. I knew the war theme was a bit intense, but I loved the historical aspect of it. (In truth, this was also pre-inauguration planning, before I had actually seen the room in person.) I proposed a design scheme that included pictures of the room with the Kennedy paper and was momentarily crestfallen when word came back that the Obamas would prefer to not sit down to family dinner every night surrounded by battle scenes.

In retrospect, my backup plan turned out to be more interesting and better suited to their needs and the large volume of the space. I had the idea that covering the walls in a classic wide stripe—I custom-printed linen in two tones of cerulean blue—would make the room warmer and more inviting. It would also help to compress the space, accentuating its elegant scale and the surprising height of its ceilings. I found a beautiful saffron crewelwork linen from Lee Jofa for the curtains, and its rich spice colors complemented the strong blues of the walls. To give the room a less formal feeling, we added a seating area in between the windows with a comfortable sofa and a Billy Baldwin slipper chair covered in chenille. The room's Teddy Roosevelt–era mahogany table was illuminated by an elaborate crystal chandelier that had been in place for years, and I commissioned a suite of carnelian-red leather dining chairs that we based on a 19th-century original. The Obamas purchased the

ABOVE: A mix of blues and spice colors complement the bold art showcased in the room. The saffron crewelwork linen is by Lee Jofa, and the wide blue stripe was custom made. OPPOSITE: One of our early renderings.

chairs as part of their decoration plan and liked them so much—they are very comfortable—they're now putting them to use in their Washington, D.C., house.

Because Michelle Obama shares my penchant for mixing high style with things far more humble, the gilded, ornately carved mirror installed over the marble mantel was sometimes offset by a trio of metal candleholders that I found at Pottery Barn. They looked like minimalist sculptures. But the most significant and meaningful aspect of the room, by far, was the juxtaposition of the impactful art we hung over the 18th-century sideboards that anchored the space—a trio of Robert Mangold shapes at left and a vibrant pair of Josef Albers oils on the right. A graceful Edgar Degas sculpture stood beside the Albers works, and two moody, lyrical canvases by Pat Steir were displayed over the sofa.

This was literally the Obama family dining room, a place where the president and first lady were deeply disciplined about sitting down to dinner with their daughters at 6:30 P.M. whenever possible, where they would mindfully review "roses and thorns"—the high and

MICHAEL S SMITH INTERIORS
ILLUSTRATION / MARK MATUSZAK

DINING ROOM (B)
1600 PENNSYLVANIA AVENUE
WASHINGTON, DC

NOVEMBER 10, 2009

low points of the day. They also hosted small gatherings for political leaders and often invited close friends and family for seated dinners. James and I were part of a group they put together one evening featuring a range of personalities from different walks of life. Though by then I was somewhat used to being in those rooms, it was intoxicating to see them appreciated by others with such a sense of awe and wonder—and to see how the president and first lady put everyone at ease with such grace. My design for their dining room reflected their enlightened aesthetic, with one foot rooted in the tradition and history of the building—so respectful of the architecture and the sense of gravitas and ceremony of the White House—and the other celebrating the color, vibrancy, and creativity of American art, a point of view that was very much of our time.

OPPOSITE: The Family Dining Room is filled with painterly northern light throughout the day. Robert Mangold's works, *½ W Series*, *½ V Series*, and *½ X Series*, hang above a late-18th-century English mahogany sideboard; the turn-of-the-century tea service is gilded silver, and the ceramic lamps are by Christopher Spitzmiller. ABOVE: From top, paintings by Pat Steir, *After Winslow Homer I* and *Waterfall with Rose Petals*, are displayed in between the windows. The artworks were on loan from the National Gallery of Art. FOLLOWING PAGES: The circa-1902 pedestal dining table was made for President Theodore Roosevelt, with a mahogany top made in 2005 by Mack S. Headley & Sons. I paired the table with leather chesterfield dining chairs adapted from my Jasper line. The curtains are of a crewel-embroidered saffron linen by Lee Jofa, and the walls were upholstered by J. C. Landa in a wide stripe by Jasper Fabrics. Mitchell Denburg made the handwoven wool-and-sisal rug.

THIRD FLOOR CORRIDOR,
MARIAN ROBINSON'S SUITE, SOLARIUM

The third floor serves a myriad of purposes. There are some 20 rooms, from a gym and a games room to several guest suites, storerooms, the Solarium, and a suite where Mrs. Obama's mother, Marian Robinson, lived. First Lady Laura Bush had refreshed many of the rooms not long before — the Billiard Room, for example, was in terrific shape, and we left it virtually untouched except to hang some art and memorabilia the president had acquired on the campaign trail. A wide hall runs nearly the length of the floor, which we updated with some classic Billy Baldwin upholstery and Ralph Pucci glass-and-steel coffee tables. The absence of any natural light made decorating the space a challenge but gave me the opportunity to borrow a series of photographs by my friend, the artist Catherine Opie. (Photographs can be on display for only a limited time in spaces with abundant light.) Catherine's striking images of Lake Michigan, on loan from the Museum of Contemporary Art Chicago, were reminders of the Obamas' hometown, but they also made the space feel light and open, almost having the effect of a window. We also mounted a large Jules Olitski canvas by the Solarium and bright, colorful paintings by William H. Johnson over a desk near the elevator, a buoyant welcome as you entered the room.

The day the Obama family arrived, Marian Robinson moved in as well. I've long admired her quiet strength and emotional intelligence; everyone looked to her as a constant source of sage advice, and she was a big favorite of the Residence staff. Her suite featured beautiful antiques and had been recently redone by Mrs. Bush, so there was little to do but rearrange some of the furniture and add pretty floral Ralph Lauren bedding to complement the stately bed. She had an elegant sitting room and the Solarium was located adjacent to her rooms, up a ramp lined with framed family photos. It has a kitchenette, and she often had her breakfast there. Though Mrs. Robinson had her privacy and independence, she was extremely involved with her granddaughters and constantly available; her cheerful presence was always deeply felt.

The Solarium is the largest and most prominent space on the third floor, situated directly above the Yellow Oval Room and offering a beautiful view south to the Washington Monument.

OPPOSITE: Photographs from Catherine Opie's *Fall, Winter, Spring, Summer (Lake Michigan)* series were installed in the Third Floor Corridor; O. Henry House made the sofa and slipper chair, and the coffee table is by Ralph Pucci.

PREVIOUS PAGES: The wide hall stretches nearly the length of the third floor. *Jean Harlow's Night, Black and Blue*, a canvas by Jules Olitski from the Museum of Contemporary Art Chicago, hangs at left, and a late-18th-century girandole mirror is displayed over the sofa at right. ABOVE AND RIGHT: Though the third floor, constructed from former attic space during the Coolidge administration renovation in 1927, features smaller windows than the lower floors, Marian Robinson's suite had been recently refreshed by First Lady Laura Bush and felt light and airy. A set of 1850s Currier & Ives floral prints flank an early-19th-century Boston desk, which displays dessert plates from the Rutherford B. Hayes state china service. The late-18th-century English high-post bed has a painted cornice, which Mrs. Bush referenced in the matching pattern she had printed on the tester. These pieces from the White House collection had been mainstays in the room for several years; we simply rearranged some of the furniture, added a few new lamps, and brought in crisp floral bed linens.

CONRAD

Tag #8356

M. Smith 3/2/09
SK ① + photo

single bo...
2" thick

ORDER FOR "MINI 'PEACE TABLE'" — MORE CHOICES!
Please let us know your preferences) or cross to discuss. Thank you.

Giant India Rosewood
butterflies in center

MICHAEL SMITH, A

(Gold)
carpenter
and on
(bevel edges)

③ A perfect size at last!
#1028 and #1027, 1⅛" thick.

④ #09337 and #09336, ±1½" thick.
March 25 2009

Gérard

JASPER
MICHAEL S SMITH
FINE FURNITURE AND FABRICS

GLANT TEXTILES
CUTTING FOR APPROVAL
03/10/09
O # 201150

SMITH INCORPORATED
TELLURIDE SADDLE

$4,000   Yards

CUTTINGS SHOULD BE VIEWED FOR
CONSISTENT WITH THE INSTALLATION SITE

ROGERS & GOFFIGON LTD

GLANT

It was built by President William H. Taft after the Roosevelt renovation for use as a sleeping porch during steamy Washington summers, with a compact alcove kitchen added decades later. It has long served as a casual den and gathering place for first families. President Eisenhower regularly barbecued on the roof deck, which is known as the Promenade, and Mrs. Kennedy created an ad hoc schoolroom in the space for her daughter, Caroline, and the children of some friends and staff.

I had thought the Solarium would be used much more as a family room for the Obamas than it actually was, but the Family Sitting Room on the second floor was likely more convenient. When Malia and Sasha were little, they would set up tepees in there, and a few years later they would move some of the furniture out and host sleepovers for their friends. I had planned it to be super family-friendly. I designed a rug with an earthy, North Africa–inspired stripe that Patterson Flynn Martin made for us, and we installed wood Venetian blinds and striped curtains at the windows. The existing sofas were re-covered in a rust-red fabric and paired with some '70s-style leather club chairs. And Mira Nakashima crafted a beautiful freeform black-walnut coffee table, adding a special inscription to the Obamas underneath; the president now uses the table in his Obama Foundation office in Washington.

MICHAEL S SMITH INTERIORS
ILLUSTRATION / MARK MATUSZAK

SOLARIUM
1600 PENNSYLVANIA AVENUE
WASHINGTON, DC

JANUARY 12, 2009

OPPOSITE: The design scheme, including Mira Nakashima's working drawings for the table she crafted for the Obamas. Our color palette included earth tones with touches of deep red. ABOVE: Our rendering. FOLLOWING PAGES: The Solarium is wrapped by windows and faces south, offering a spectacular view of the Washington Monument.

FAMILY SITTING ROOM

Given its location adjacent to the Master Bedroom and the president's bathroom, the role of this room transitions back and forth from the president's bedroom—when the president and first lady keep separate sleeping quarters—to a living room, a private study, and a den (Laura Bush often referred to it as their puzzle room). It's also adjacent to the Yellow Oval Room, though the connecting door is seldom used and, in some cases, has been blocked by furniture.

Since the Obamas would share the Master Bedroom, we had the perfect opportunity to create a great American family room—one that happens to overlook the Washington Monument, but a family room nonetheless. It was a space with a large television, and it was across the hall from the girls' rooms, so it ended up being everyone's go-to room to relax. It is generously sized, as are nearly all the rooms on this floor, and features 12-foot ceilings and elaborate architectural detail. In an effort to lessen its formality, I covered the walls with a handwoven, spice-colored grass cloth that we had embroidered in a subtle arabesque pattern to add a layer of texture. The wallpaper's dusky palette almost gave the effect of a paneled room. I installed a sculptural wood, bronze, and glass chandelier by Pagani Studio—it was like a mobile and reminded me

a bit of George Nakashima's work, which was vastly different from the traditional fixtures in the Residence—and I grounded the space with an aubergine patterned rug I designed for

OPPOSITE: Sean Scully's painting *ONEONEZERONINE RED*, on loan from the National Gallery of Art, is displayed against a wall clad in a rush-cloth paper by Crezana. The sofa is by Roman Thomas, the side pedestal table and travertine-top table are by Jasper Furniture, and the rug is by Mansour. ABOVE: The chandelier is by PaganiStudio, the gilt-wood mirror is early 19th century, and the painting on the far right is Glenn Ligon's *Black Like Me #2*, from the Hirshhorn Museum. The sofas and leather wing chairs are by Roman Thomas.

Mansour. We mixed sofas and wing chairs by Roman Thomas (a New York–based furniture maker known for reductive versions of classic American forms) with circa-1902 side chairs from the White House collection and an 18th-century Pennsylvania high chest that formerly stood against the window wall when this room served as President Kennedy's bedroom. Through various administrations, the tall chest had been moved in and out of the space, but as it was the first significant piece of fine furniture donated to Jacqueline Kennedy's restoration project, I felt it was essential here.

With its views over the South Lawn, this room always seemed particularly American to me. I wanted to amplify that sense by installing quintessential American art, including large paintings by Glenn Ligon and Sean Scully, plus works by Louise Nevelson and Jasper Johns that we displayed between the windows. And though it worked well as a family space,

ABOVE: Stripes and textures for pillows contrast with neutrals for upholstery and saffron linen for the curtains. OPPOSITE: An early rendering that we updated a few times before installation. FOLLOWING PAGES: A late-18th-century Pennsylvania high chest stands at far left. Louise Nevelson's painting *Model for Sky Covenant* hangs above *Numerals, 0 through 9*, a lead relief by Jasper Johns; both were loaned by the National Gallery.

this interior was also the most expressive of the Obamas' personal taste. It was important for me to interweave pieces of iconic American furniture with work by influential contemporary artists who had great meaning to them. This room best reflects the overall Obama aesthetic—a mindful, gentle blending of historical antiques and architecture with 20th- and 21st-century art and furnishings. All of these pieces were individually strong, but when we brought them together, when they coalesced, they helped set the narrative for what this first family's life in the White House might signify. In a very real way, as I planned this room it served as the laboratory for the president's Oval Office, which I installed in late summer of the following year, as well as a template for the style imprint of the Obama years.

My goal was to help as the Obama administration navigated the White House into a new era of openness and creative inclusivity, to have reverence and respect for historic precedence yet to embrace the texture, color, and fresh new voices that were more representative of the country at this point in time. This room reflected a way forward. And today, all of the furnishings Michelle and Barack Obama purchased for this space more than a decade ago have taken on a new life in their Washington, D.C., house. For even as the president and first lady thoughtfully referenced the past, they always anticipated the future.

MICHAEL S SMITH INTERIORS
ILLUSTRATION / MARK MATUSZAK

FAMILY SITTING ROOM
1600 PENNSYLVANIA AVENUE
WASHINGTON, DC

MARCH 10, 2009

TREATY ROOM

The Treaty Room was one of the most fascinating spaces in the White House. I designed it to be Barack Obama's personal retreat, and other than the Oval Office and his private study in the West Wing, it's where the president spent the most time—conferring with his staff before Cabinet meetings or on weekends and habitually working late into the night. In fact, the one time I was fortunate to sleep over at the Residence after an official trip to Europe with the president, following a nine-hour flight from Spain he stayed in the Treaty Room until 3 A.M., reading his briefing books. This room was where he would often work after early dinners with his family and where he read the ten constituent letters his staff selected for him every day. On the rare occasion he had a chance to relax, it's where he would watch basketball games. But most important, for this perpetual student and Socratic thinker, it was his place for research and contemplation. I felt it was essential that it not only reflect his spirit and

OPPOSITE: A series of scenes of Native American life by George Catlin, on loan from the National Gallery of Art, hang above a mid-19th-century table crafted in Baltimore. ABOVE: A collection of challenge coins, the commemorative medals given to President Obama by different units of the military.

character, but also reference the warm design aesthetic of his Craftsman-style interiors in Chicago. I wanted this space to be the crossover point between the past and present.

Before the West Wing was built, for many years the room served as the Cabinet Room, and President Obama chose President Ulysses S. Grant's Victorian-era cabinet table to use as his desk—it has eight locking drawers, one for each Cabinet member to store important papers— and several treaties were signed on it, including the 1898 peace protocol which led to the end of the Spanish-American War. Jacqueline Kennedy's decision to rename this space the Treaty Room (formerly the Monroe Room) was inspired by the diplomatic agreements negotiated here.

ABOVE: The room's palette was rich yet subtle. OPPOSITE: The rendering illustrates the painterly appeal of the stenciled frieze. FOLLOWING PAGES: The walls were clad in a Larsen abaca paper with a Native American motif stenciled as a border. The gilded mirror is mid-19th century, and the velvet curtains were installed during the George W. Bush administration. I repositioned the president's desk between the windows; it was a mid-19th-century conference table which had been used to sign several international treaties.

I always felt a great sense of history in this room and very much associated it with the age of expansion and the great American West. I covered the walls with a woven-abaca paper by Larsen and had a Native American motif stenciled as a frieze; it connected the millwork with the rest of the room and made it less formal. We repositioned POTUS's desk between the windows, creating an additional seating area where it formerly stood, and when President Bush's lush green velvet curtains shrank during cleaning, I took the opportunity to add a contrasting border. We displayed a series of George Catlin's iconic, late-19th-century oil paintings to flank the fireplace, ranging from Buffalo Bill to scenes of the Great Plains, and on the opposite wall I hung *Butterfly*, a contemporary painting by Susan Rothenberg, an American artist who lives in New Mexico with her husband, the artist Bruce Nauman. It was another connection with the West, and she is a great talent whose work had not been showcased in the White House. Photos of this room often included the Rothenberg, and the painting became emblematic of its style and design.

MICHAEL S SMITH INTERIORS
ILLUSTRATION / MARK MATUSZAK

TREATY ROOM
1600 PENNSYLVANIA AVENUE
WASHINGTON, DC

MARCH 10, 2009

FROM TOP: The president often worked late into the night after an early dinner with his family. Personal mementos, including a football inscribed to the president by military aides, were grouped along the mantel.

174

FROM TOP: President Obama meeting with national-security aides John Brennan (*foreground*) and Denis McDonough in 2011; the painting is Susan Rothenberg's *Butterfly*, on loan from the National Gallery. The president watches Michelle Obama deliver her September 2012 Democratic National Convention speech with Malia (*left*) and Sasha.

RIGHT: In the entrance to the Treaty Room from the East Hall are portraits of presidents George Washington, by an unknown artist (*top left*), and Ulysses S. Grant, by Thomas LeClear (*bottom left*), above a bronze bust of Sir Winston Churchill by Jacob Epstein that was given to President Lyndon Johnson in 1965. (A second Epstein bust of Sir Winston, loaned to George W. Bush by Prime Minister Tony Blair while this bust was under repair, had been on display in the Oval Office. It was returned, as promised, when President Bush left office.) On the right, *Washington's Tomb at Mount Vernon*, by William Matthew Prior, and *U.S. Capitol*, by an unknown artist, hang above a cast-metal sculpture of Major General Andrew Jackson, a miniature version of the celebrated Lafayette Park statue. The mahogany tables are early 19th century, a gift of the White House acquisition fund. By tradition, the U.S. flag is displayed on the left and the flag of the President of the United States is on the right; the flagpoles are crowned with polished-brass eagles.

WEST SITTING HALL AND CENTER HALL

At the west end of the Center Hall, there is a welcoming seating area under one of the Residence's signature half-moon windows. Located between the Family Dining Room on the north side and the Master Bedroom suite on the south, it's a generously sized space, decorated less formally than the Yellow Oval Room but not as low-key as the Family Sitting Room. I remember finding a photo of Nancy Reagan smiling as she posed on the floor, appearing to wrap Christmas presents, just a few pages from an image of her with President Reagan, sharing cocktails with Prince Charles and Princess Diana on the sofa under the window. For the Obamas, as with the Reagans, the West Sitting Hall served as their de facto living room.

The Bushes' subtle design scheme worked well, though we re-covered the sofas and chairs and added a few modern, clean-lined pieces by furniture maker Roman Thomas. I had commissioned a pair of plaster Queen Anne–style side tables from the artisan Stephen Antonson—inspired by an antique table, I loved the surprise of that classic curvaceous silhouette executed in a chalky plaster. Perfect for this space, they were among some of the pieces I found it easier to simply loan to the Obama White House. Because of the president and first lady's great interest in art, we displayed a range of different works borrowed from museums, except for a tranquil Claude Monet landscape, which has hung to the right of the window for years. A gift to the White House from the Kennedy family in honor of President John F. Kennedy following his assassination, it would be inconceivable to move it.

These walls and those of the Center Hall were painted a taupe-putty color as a neutral background for works we borrowed from the National Gallery and the Hirshhorn. Alma Thomas's vibrant *Sky Light* was installed next to the Family Dining Room, and on a visit a few years ago, not long after the holidays, I was thrilled that the turntable and speakers I had given the

OPPOSITE: The West Sitting Hall, with its distinctive half-moon window, is located between the Family Dining Room and the Master Bedroom suite. We re-covered the existing sofas and chairs, and I commissioned artisan Stephen Antonson to craft a pair of plaster Queen Anne–style side tables based on an antique I spotted at auction. The Claude Monet landscape, *Morning on the Seine, Good Weather*, was a gift to the White House from the Kennedy family in memory of President John F. Kennedy.

president for Christmas were being used atop a pier table under the Thomas painting and the collection of albums I gave him already had new additions. Seeing the juxtaposition of the music playing near that joyful painting just made me happy.

The adjacent Center Hall runs like a river through the middle of the floor, with the East and West Sitting Halls at either end and all rooms in between leading from it. A windowless space that measures about 64 feet long and 18 feet wide, with very tall ceilings, it's a cross be-

tween no-man's-land and the true heart of the house. It's traditionally been treated as more of a circulation space, likely because of the lighting situation. With literally no natural light, the space had muted illumination from crystal chandeliers and spots of bright light from a scattering of table and floor lamps, creating dark corners and gloomy shadows. I vowed to upgrade the lighting with inset ceiling fixtures as soon as it was feasible, as it was exactly the type of project that was important to Mrs. Obama—what improvements can we make to help future first families?

In the meantime, I worked to create a more fun, functional design—formal enough to usher world leaders through on their way to the Yellow Oval Room, yet comfortable enough for the president, first lady, and Mrs. Robinson to sit and listen to the girls play the piano. It was essential to respect past history and precedence while infusing the space with a sense of American ease and warmth. We formed a few seating areas with classic 1960s-style upholstery and a vintage Pace Collection coffee table. The pale carpet was timeworn, so we had three subtly patterned rugs made by Patterson Flynn Martin that were relatively impervious to both young children and rambunctious pets. I brought in a pair of glazed-stoneware urns and pedestals by Peter Schlesinger to flank the door to the East Sitting Hall, and although

ABOVE: An Alma Thomas painting, *Sky Light*, on loan from the Hirshhorn Museum and Sculpture Garden, is displayed over a late-19th-century English pier table. I gave the turntable, speakers, and some of the albums to the president as a Christmas present. OPPOSITE: Our rendering for the space.

the president wasn't particularly keen on them—he would never say he didn't like something; it would be a graceful "they're not my taste"—I like to think he grew to appreciate the nod to historic forms yet modern presence they added to the space. The most important addition was the art—we relocated Ed Ruscha's red canvas from move-in day, *I Think I'll…*, from one wall to another and flanked the entrance to the Yellow Oval Room with Hans Hofmann's *Staccato in Blue* and *White Line*, by Sam Francis, both from the National Gallery of Art.

Though there were major hurdles and many obstacles to my lighting project, I was persistent, and with Bill Allman's help and the support of Mrs. Obama, we developed a plan to add recessed LED ceiling lights to the Center Hall, the Family Dining Room, and a few other rooms. In August, when the first family left for their summer vacation, our team of experts—led by Bob Truax of Truax Design Group and Bob Clark of Clayco—sprang into action, as the project would require a few days of concentrated work and a great deal of disruption within the Residence. This modern intervention in the historic house not only banished its shadows and gloom, it also enabled us to direct warm beams of light on the extraordinary art on loan from the national museums. These rooms, now filled with clear, beautiful light, were not only more livable and more welcoming, they were, at last, literally more artful.

MICHAEL S SMITH INTERIORS
ILLUSTRATION / MARK MATUSZAK

WEST SITTING HALL
1600 PENNSYLVANIA AVENUE
WASHINGTON, DC

AUGUST 12, 2011

OPPOSITE: Installing LED ceiling lights in the Second Floor Center Hall was not an easy task, but expert teams led by Bob Truax of Truax Design Group and Bob Clark of Clayco were trusted pros. So as not to be disruptive, extensive renovation work was always undertaken during the family's two annual holidays. ABOVE: Ed Ruscha's canvas *I Think I'll…* is displayed in the foreground (it was originally placed on the right, above the sofa). Before we installed the ceiling lights in the Center Hall, the cavernous space was filled with shadows offset by spots of light from scattered table lamps. RIGHT: I was so taken with this glazed-stoneware urn and pedestal by artist and photographer Peter Schlesinger that I loaned the Obamas a pair to flank the door to the East Hall. FOLLOWING PAGES: The new ceiling fixtures cast a consistent light throughout the space. Hans Hofmann's *Staccato in Blue* is displayed on the far wall and *White Line*, by Sam Francis, hangs in the foreground, both on loan from the National Gallery of Art. The sofa and armchair are by O. Henry House, and the coffee table is a 1970s Pace Collection design; the carpets are by Patterson Flynn Martin. The mahogany partners desk in the center of the room is mid-18th-century English, and the piano is by Steinway & Sons.

YELLOW OVAL ROOM

For me, one of the most beautiful and romantic places in the White House is the Yellow Oval Room. I've always thought of it as the most emblematic of Jacqueline Kennedy and her flawless interpretation of classic American style—albeit with a nod to European inspiration. As the space is built directly over the Blue Room on the State Floor, it replicates its scale, proportions, and graceful oval shape, and it's the most heroic of the upstairs private rooms, with windows that look out over the Truman Balcony, past the sweeping expanse of the South Lawn to the iconic Washington Monument in the distance.

The Yellow Oval has exquisite features—a distinctive geometry, soaring ceilings, a striking neoclassical chimneypiece, and refined architectural detail. I did an enormous amount of research on it, reviewing notes and photos of its previous incarnations. Mrs. Kennedy particularly loved the room and worked diligently to make it worldly and sophisticated, securing funding for its restoration from philanthropic supporters and significant donations of prized pieces from a myriad of generous friends, including a stunning 18th-century desk that remains an elegant anchor as you enter the space.

Another highlight for me was First Lady Nancy Reagan's version of the Yellow Oval, which was a lovely, formal space with dramatically detailed curtains, the glow of soft lighting, and many of the Reagans' personal objects and furniture. They entertained regularly, and the room was in constant use—I think they hosted more than 50 state dinners during their two terms.

At the time President and Mrs. Obama moved in, there were two generously sized sofas and coffee tables flanking the marble mantel, with a scattering of comfortable chairs. We

OPPOSITE: While honoring the legacy of the Yellow Oval Room, we also incorporated modern designs, such as gold-leafed cast-glass tables by Magni Home Collection and ceramic table lamps by Christopher Spitzmiller.

decided that a looser floor plan with the addition of more seating areas would create a space that was stately yet slightly less formal. This would be the room where the president and first lady would serve guests drinks before a dinner party, as well as where world leaders, ambassadors, and other dignitaries would gather for a private moment with the Obamas prior to a State Dinner. It needed to have the formal feeling of a drawing room because it was a semipublic space, but the family would also use it as their living room — for example, it's where their personal Christmas tree would be set up during the holidays.

Over its two centuries, the room had served many functions — as a parlor, an office, a library, etc. — and survived a series of decorating permutations. However, when Mrs. Kennedy transformed it from President Dwight Eisenhower's study and trophy room into a sophisticated living room, she painted it a pale yellow hue that has remained synonymous with the space to this day. Nancy Reagan preferred a lemony yellow, but I thought it should be a richer color — one famously described by Virginia-born English decorator Nancy Lancaster as "buttah yellow." Yellow can be a challenging color to work with, and it's not easy to find

ABOVE: One of the early renderings of the room by Mark Matuszak. OPPOSITE: Post-meeting markups and notes; the furniture plan was still in flux, and we proposed a few curtain options before finalizing.

the right one, but after a lengthy consultation with color expert Donald Kaufman, we came up with a perfect shade; it had a touch of apricot. As with everything I did in the White House, I had gone into full obsession mode, thinking of all of the different fabrics and wallpapers that might work on the walls, but it ended up being far more practical to do paint.

I also focused on the floor, as few of the carpets in the White House collection fit the room, and I thought the ones that did weren't strong enough to act as a proper foundation to ground the space. Miraculously, I found a large antique Oushak at auction. Although too big, when the rug was trimmed and laid in the room, the green and yellow combination worked beautifully — it seemed to reflect the sky and garden beyond the windows, and I decided to donate it to the White House collection as an official gift, which I soon learned has a very formal protocol.

The curtains, lined in a blue-and-white silk, are a modification of a design proposed by Stéphane Boudin; though they were never realized when he was working with Jackie Kennedy, it seemed an appropriate source of inspiration. This room always felt to me as if it were meant

to be an American interpretation of a French room. However, it was also essential to have elements of modernity in the space, which we added with a pair of jewellike, gilded cast-glass coffee tables. We also brought in Tony Duquette ostrich-egg candlesticks and hurricane lamps by Frederick P. Victoria (a favorite source of Mrs. Kennedy), and I commissioned a custom-made overmantel mirror based on a Federal design. We kept a simple mahogany pedestal table in front of the window for dining or to enjoy the open view, and though Bill Allman and I searched, we couldn't find White House chairs to pair with it. At an auction in London, I came across a set of well-priced Louis XVI chairs that were perfect—an homage to both Kennedy and Obama style—which I purchased and donated to the collection.

One of my first steps had been to commission new sofas from Jonas, a New York firm that has crafted upholstery for the White House since the Kennedy years, and we covered them in a watery blue-green silk damask; it's a color that I somehow always associate with Michelle Obama. We upholstered the bergères in a chestnut silk velvet; given to the White House during the Kennedy restoration, I think they had been in storage since perhaps the Ford era.

As in many White House rooms, there are inset shelves where Chinese export plates were displayed. The president was very clear that he didn't understand the reasoning behind using plates as decoration, something I happen to agree with. The Prime Minister of India was coming for the Obamas' first State Dinner, and I racked my brain thinking of what might be appropriate to display on the shelves that would be reflective of America. Crazily, I remembered that Sears, Roebuck & Co. had donated a collection of antique children's cast-iron toys to the Smithsonian, including a variety of train replicas. I had this notion from an English novel that described India as a country of trains, and I decided they might be appropriate. It turned out there weren't enough trains, so we also requested fire and police trucks and merchants' carts, all miniature examples of American ingenuity and commerce. In the end, I was told everyone thought the toys were wonderful, not only interesting and thought-provoking but quite beautiful, and they stayed in place for the duration of the presidency.

We also borrowed a number of paintings over the years, and other works got moved around as some needed to be returned for public exhibition. For a while there were some incredible Barnett Newmans, an Alice Neel, and there were two beautiful Cézannes from the White House collection. I believed that if any room in the Residence should be Jeffersonian—the idea that it was inhabited by someone who went to Europe and returned with wonderful things—it was the Yellow Oval Room. This became a favorite room of the Obamas for both public and private use, and I loved thinking that the president, who came to the White House a bit of a modernist, had developed a greater appreciation for the beauty and impact of rooms that were classic, perhaps even traditional. For the president and first lady, I wanted to make the Yellow Oval Room the very best version of itself.

OPPOSITE: Our palette was built on one created by Jacqueline Kennedy in the early 1960s. ABOVE, FROM LEFT: The color yellow comprises a range of hues; we worked with master colorist Donald Kaufman to determine the perfect one. The Stéphane Boudin–inspired curtain design was mocked up in silk taffeta.

PREVIOUS PAGES: Paintings by Paul Cézanne (*left*) and Daniel Garber from the White House collection flank the fireplace, and antique toys from the Smithsonian are displayed on the shelves to the left; the Jonas sofas are covered in a Claremont damask. ABOVE, FROM TOP: The Obamas hosted a 2010 dinner with President Nicolas Sarkozy of France and his wife, Carla Bruni. President and Mrs. Obama with President François Hollande before the France State Dinner in 2014.

ABOVE, FROM TOP: Prior to their final State Dinner in October 2016, President and Mrs. Obama met with Italian Prime Minister Matteo Renzi and his wife, Agnese Landini. One month later, the Obamas hosted a private dinner for Senate Minority Leader Harry Reid and his wife, Landra, seated to the left of President Obama; on the right are Senator Charles Schumer and his wife, Iris Weinshall. FOLLOWING PAGES: The Denis-Louis Ancellet writing table in the foreground is late 18th century; paintings by Paul Jon Wonner from the Hirshhorn Museum are hung to the right of the windows.

6   WHITE HOUSE OFFICES AND STATE ROOMS

I realized long ago that the difference between furnishing and decorating is emotional connectivity. I say all the time that the best rooms are essentially portraiture, and a wonderful thing about the Obama White House was that it truly reflected who they are — their extraordinary curiosity, their warm embrace of all cultures and creeds, and their striking authenticity. The design decisions they made, from furnishing their offices to refreshing official public spaces, were particularly mindful of the fact that the country was struggling through a financial crisis. Every decision, every change had meaning and exemplified their mission to celebrate the best of America, to make the White House more open and accessible to all — and to honor its history while doing everything possible to prepare it for the future.

When I wasn't in Washington, though I felt I lived there — and actually did during the summer of 2013, after my partner, James, was appointed ambassador to Spain and Andorra and was in State Department training in Virginia — I was focused on my bustling L.A. design office and showroom. Yet the president and Mrs. Obama were never far from my mind, and I was always seeking ways to make their spaces, both public and private, as warm and welcoming as possible. Bill Allman once said that my greatest success was how comfortable the first family was and how quickly I transformed their private quarters into a home that was personal and full of life. I was thrilled, but also acutely conscious that those rooms were primarily seen only by close friends, as Mrs. Obama was deeply committed to keeping family and public life separate; even visits by senior staff were few and far between.

It was essential that spaces open to the public also reflected the Obamas' cultural mindset and love of art and design. The first lady's initial approach to State Floor projects was always with a sense of pragmatism, as she was very attentive to improving how rooms might function for future administrations. She was also super interested in the refurbish-

OPPOSITE: Walking with President Obama along the West Colonnade that leads from the Residence to the Oval Office in the West Wing. The president's daily commute usually took less than two minutes.

ment of State Rooms included on the public tour, working in tandem with Bill Allman, the WHHA, and the Committee for the Preservation of the White House. Our primary projects on the State Floor were the ongoing restoration of the Monroe-era Bellangé suite of furnishings; refreshing the curtains, chairs, and carpet in the State Dining Room; and transforming the Old Family Dining Room into a groundbreaking showcase for contemporary art. Her passion and spirit elevated all aspects of any project we took on.

President Obama's approach was somewhat different. He is basically a modernist and at one point even considered becoming an architect. He has a deep thirst for knowledge and was always interested in the details and historic reference points of everything in the house. In truth, the design of his Oval Office had been in the back of my mind from the outset. It is the most personal and symbolic of White House rooms—literally the apex of power in America. But barely a month post-inauguration, my heart sank when remarks the president made regarding the federal budget hit the news cycle and one line jumped out: "There are times where you can afford to redecorate your house, and there are times where you need to focus on rebuilding its foundation." The Oval Office project was back-burnered for well over a year.

There was a lot to do in the meantime, in addition to our continuing work in the Residence. My friend Alyssa Mastromonaco, one of the president's deputy chiefs of staff, once described the West Wing as "a lot like you see on TV, except much older and more worn out." We updated run-down areas scheduled for a refresh and did a modest redo of the first lady's East Wing office. Then, in the late summer of 2010, we finally installed the new Oval Office. The reaction was intense, to say the least. All of a sudden, everyone was a design expert. Even Alyssa admitted she wasn't sure about the wallpaper at first but described the office as "amazing" when it was done. She said, "Everyone prior had tried to make the Oval Office look like Jefferson was still working there." ABC-TV newsman George Stephanopoulos, a former Clinton White House staffer (and a close friend), commented that I had "brought the Oval Office into the 21st century. The minute you saw it, you knew it was paying obvious respect to tradition, but modernizing it. It was unmistakably Obama."

My favorite description, however, was that of *Washington Post* columnist Sally Quinn in a *New York Times* feature: "Bush's room says, 'Let's have a glass of wine while we sign the treaty.' Obama's room says, 'This is serious. We don't have time to waste. Double espresso, anyone?' The message is this: whoever is in that office has the most stressful job in the world. Whatever it takes to lessen the pressure and create a calmer and more relaxed atmosphere is the only thing that matters."

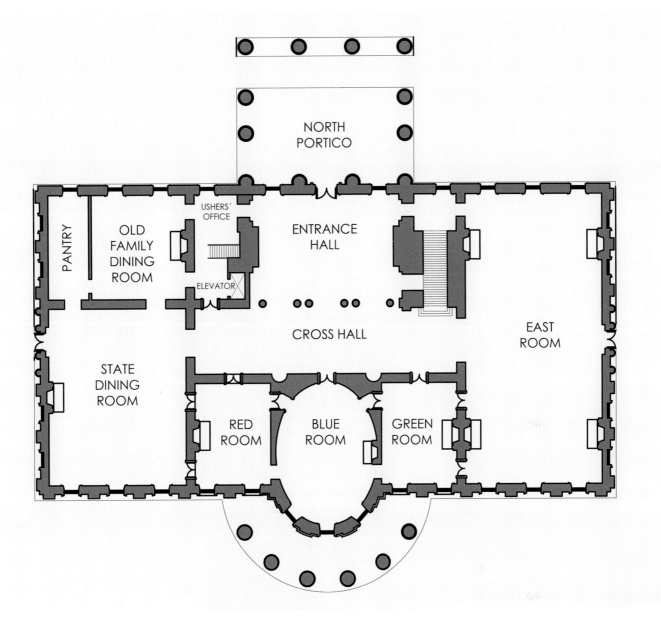

NORTH
PORTICO

PANTRY

OLD
FAMILY
DINING
ROOM

USHERS'
OFFICE

ELEVATOR

ENTRANCE
HALL

EAST
ROOM

CROSS HALL

STATE
DINING
ROOM

RED
ROOM

BLUE
ROOM

GREEN
ROOM

ABOVE: The plan for the first floor of the Residence, known as the State Floor, shows the layout of the formal State Rooms, including the Entrance Hall, which leads from the North Portico, and the Cross Hall, extending from the East Room across to the State Dining Room. The main reception rooms are contiguous, with the State Dining Room opening to the Red Room, which leads to the oval Blue Room, the Green Room, and the East Room, the largest space. The Old Family Dining Room, often used as a staging area for large events, was redecorated by the Obamas in 2015 to showcase contemporary art and added to the rooms featured on the official public tour. RIGHT: During August 2009, a White House worker perched on tall scaffolding brushing a fresh coat of white paint on the walls of the Cross Hall while the first family was away on summer vacation.

FIRST LADY MICHELLE OBAMA'S OFFICE

Not long after our progress on the family quarters was underway, I received a call that various halls in the West Wing needed attention, as well as in the East Wing, where the offices for the first lady and her staff are located. To be honest, the East Wing offices never receive much public focus. Though home to a large and extremely busy staff, they are rarely seen by the outside world. Some of the compact, utilitarian spaces were looking a bit timeworn—traditionally, both wings receive a refresh every six or seven years, and apparently it was overdue.

The reception areas and halls must withstand constant use, as scores of visitors arrive for meetings on a daily basis. While we repainted and installed new wallpaper and carpets as needed, we were also tasked with updating the first lady's office to suit her style of working. Michelle Obama's program agenda was already in full swing, as she had arrived on Inauguration Day with many of her team vetted and in place. I think there were eventually around 20 people on her staff—from policy directors to schedulers to press secretaries—as well as the social secretary and events team, including the White House's expert calligraphy staff, who also fell under the first lady's purview (and office space).

FLOTUS worked everywhere—hosting events, visiting schools and community programs, spending time at military and veterans hospitals, and constantly traveling, in addition to creating the celebrated White House Kitchen Garden and spearheading her signature programs. She held meetings here to strategize her initiatives, but she also worked from her office in the Residence to be close to her children when they arrived home from school. So it was essential to the first lady that her formal office be designed as multipurpose and put to use for meetings by everyone on her staff.

OPPOSITE: For her East Wing office, Michelle Obama opted for a conference table instead of a desk, which we paired with Chippendale-style chairs. The walls were painted a glazed custom-mixed terra-cotta.

MICHAEL S SMITH INTERIORS
ILLUSTRATION / MARK MATUSZAK

FIRST LADY'S OFFICE (A)
1600 PENNSYLVANIA AVENUE
WASHINGTON, DC

FEBRUARY 5, 2009

Our first move was to replace the desk with a long conference table surrounded by a fleet of Chippendale–style chairs that Bill Allman helped me find. I painted the walls in layers of a soft terra-cotta color topped with a subtle glaze. Ceilings are often a missed opportunity, and I installed gridded acoustical millwork, enabling us to add more lighting, while tall white shutters provided privacy and filtered sunlight when needed for photo shoots. The primary seating included a pair of deeply cushioned spool chairs and a classic sofa in a sturdy chevron twill, all by Hickory Chair.

We hung an Ellsworth Kelly sculpture on one wall and had our hearts set on a beautiful, nearly square Alma Thomas canvas for between the windows, but it had to be installed close to the ceiling and ended up being too overscale for the space. The press went wild, alleging a controversy that the painting was returned because it too closely mimicked an Henri Matisse work, but it was actually merely a size issue; although we loved it, it overwhelmed the room. We were able to borrow a dramatic Mark Rothko from the National Gallery to take its place.

This office might have been designed to work for FLOTUS's team, but it grew even more personal for Mrs. Obama over the eight years, as favorite books filled the shelves and family photos and special collections were grouped on tabletops. And I'll always have incredible memories of our meetings in that serene spot in the whirlwind of the East Wing.

OPPOSITE, FROM TOP: An early rendering. The design scheme was Billy Baldwin–inspired, including a mix of graphic prints and toss pillows from my Jasper line of fabrics. ABOVE: We were excited by the Hirshhorn Museum's loan of Alma Thomas's *Watusi (Hard Edge)*, but it proved too large for the space. A painted-aluminum work from Ellsworth Kelly's *Painted Wall Sculptures* series from the National Gallery is displayed on the adjacent wall.

LEFT: Michelle Obama engaged in a scheduled Twitter chat, discussing her school-nutrition initiative and the White House Kitchen Garden. BELOW: In a planning meeting for Joining Forces—the program launched by the first lady and Dr. Jill Biden to support service members, veterans, and their families—FLOTUS is shown with (*from left*) Joining Forces executive director Air Force Colonel Nicole Malachowski, Rory Brosius, Sheila Nix, and Dr. Biden. Mark Rothko's *No. 17 [or] No. 15* canvas, on loan from the National Gallery, replaced the Alma Thomas painting. OPPOSITE: Mahogany spool chairs by Hickory Chair were upholstered in a print by Pintura Studio.

OVAL OFFICE

I'll never forget walking into the Oval Office for the first time. Of course, your breath immediately catches, as the weight of history is palpable and powerful, though surprisingly the space doesn't look at all as you think it would. The room is extremely tall, oval but very vertical, and very bright—illuminated with an otherworldly fill-in light because it is camera-ready for photographers and TV crews at all times. As a student of history, even after frequent visits I never lost my sense of wonder at being there.

During the summer of 2010, we were finally able to start working on the redecoration project. Barack Obama had been president well over a year, long enough for us to ascertain how he was really using the space and what updates he wanted. It was quite clear that his was a hardworking office, not one for mere ceremony. People were in and out for meetings throughout the day and sometimes well into the evening. There was a constant focus on getting things done and moving the nation forward.

I knew the office needed to be a work space—this would be a no-drama room for a no-drama president. It had to be effective and efficient, calm enough for intense meetings but also a quiet place to read his multiple briefing books. It must be an elegant, graceful setting to receive foreign heads of state, yet also serve as a background with the gravitas necessary for televised remarks delivered during times of crisis. It wasn't the place to be showy or dramatic, and it was essential that every update we made had a personal resonance for the president. One of my first additions was an American Shaker bowl for the coffee table that I asked the staff to keep filled with apples. Not only were they healthy, but the bowl was beautiful, the gesture was welcoming, and there was a sense of utility to it. It reflected the Obama mindset.

OPPOSITE: President Obama's Oval Office, which was not updated with new furnishings and wallpaper until well into the second year of his administration; it was installed in late August of 2010.

Though the room's walls had been painted in shades of white throughout several administrations, I decided to cover them in neutral stripes to unify the space—there are multiple doors—and to add pattern and decoration without being fussy. We originally sampled stripes printed on a woven texture to reference President William Howard Taft, who created the first Oval Office and clad its walls in green burlap. Unfortunately, the fabric seemed poorly suited to wear and tear inflicted by the room's two jib doors and we pivoted to Elizabeth Dow's hand-printed stripes on a paper ground. The rigidity of the stripes was softened by a brushed wash, which gave them a painterly effect. The subtle

ABOVE: Our design incorporated warm textures and earth tones punctuated by curtains of a deep red wool and a tailored red border edging the ceiling molding and chair rail. We wanted to print the stripes on a burlap wall covering (swatch shown), but it proved problematic and we opted for wallpaper. OPPOSITE: A rendering used to present art options.

color emphasized the room's chalky white architectural detail and offered a muted background for the striking art and historic antiques.

Since the late 20th century, it's been a tradition for presidents to install a new carpet with the presidential seal. For instance, Bill Clinton's was a bright blue, and Laura Bush designed one with a sunburst of radiating stripes for George W. Bush. Keeping in mind that President Obama was not only an author but very much appreciated text in paintings and other art forms, it seemed appropriate that his carpet would be less about decorative motifs or iconography and more about the written word. He chose five quotes, from Dr. Martin Luther King, Jr. and presidents Abraham Lincoln, Theodore Roosevelt, Franklin D. Roosevelt, and John F. Kennedy, which were woven around the rug's border. Always trying to be mindful, I had a crazy idea of finding wool from different states—I even researched if there were sheep in Hawaii—but I learned that almost all custom-made rugs are woven of New Zealand wool because it is the most durable and long-lasting. President Obama's

MICHAEL S SMITH INTERIORS
ILLUSTRATION / MARK MATUSZAK

OVAL OFFICE ART OPTIONS
1600 PENNSYLVANIA AVENUE
WASHINGTON, DC

MAY 13, 2013

OPPOSITE: Children were frequent visitors to the Oval Office, including Jacob (*left*) and James Haynes, the sons of staffer Heather Foster; they posed for a selfie with the president in December 2015. LEFT: One of the images White House photographer Pete Souza shot to document the new Oval Office rug on September 1, 2010. BELOW, FROM TOP: POTUS at work at the Resolute desk. On an October 2011 visit to the Oval Office, the president shows students from Chicago's Johnson College Prep a patent model for Samuel Morse's telegraph.

MICHAEL S SMITH INTERIORS
ILLUSTRATION / MARK MATUSZAK

OVAL OFFICE RUG
1600 PENNSYLVANIA AVENUE
WASHINGTON, DC

JUNE 19, 2010

ABOVE: A rendering for our new rug, ringed with quotes meaningful to the president: "The only thing we have to fear is fear itself," by President Franklin D. Roosevelt; "The arc of the moral universe is long, but it bends towards justice," by Dr. Martin Luther King, Jr.; "Government of the people, by the people, for the people," by President Abraham Lincoln; "No problem of human destiny is beyond human beings," by President John F. Kennedy; and "The welfare of each of us is dependent fundamentally upon the welfare of all of us," by President Theodore Roosevelt.

carpet was hand-sewn in Grand Rapids, Michigan, by Scott Group Studio, using a combination of New Zealand wool and 25 percent recycled wool, and they generously donated
the monumental rug to the Obama administration.

There was no question the president would keep the Resolute desk in place, as it's the foundation of the room. I ordered custom sofas from Jonas, the New York firm that had crafted
upholstery for the White House since the Kennedy era. I covered them in a coffee-colored
linen velvet that was subtly interwoven with red, white, and blue threads. Bill Allman informed me that we needed to have three sofas in rotation for cleaning: Not only are they
in constant use during staff meetings, but when guests visit, they are often so nervous that
they rub sweaty palms on the fabric and leave marks. That is one reason why I opted for a
darker color for the upholstery, as well as the fact that many people who are excited to meet
the president have freshly polished shoes and don't realize that when they brush their feet
against the sofa skirt, it leaves marks. Without Bill Allman, this is not something I would
ever normally consider; I come from California, the land of white sofas.

The coffee table was made by artisan Roman Thomas of walnut veneered with mica in a brick
pattern, and we topped the pair of drop-leaf tables at the foot of the sofas with vivid blue

ABOVE: The press would literally swarm the Oval Office to report statements before bilateral meetings, such as this one
between POTUS and European Council President Donald Tusk in March 2015. OPPOSITE: The eagle in the presidential
seal faces away from the arrows and toward the olive branch to show that America is a nation of peace; Scott Group Studio
made the rug by hand and donated it to the White House. FOLLOWING PAGES: The Resolute desk is flanked on the left
by Edward Hopper's *Cobb's Barns, South Truro* (*top*) and *Burly Cobb's House, South Truro*, on loan from the Whitney Museum
of American Art; Childe Hassam's *The Avenue in the Rain* hangs to the right, above Frederic Remington's *The Bronco Buster*.

lamps by ceramist Christopher Spitzmiller, who had worked in the Clinton White House social office early in his career and made beautiful lamps for several of the Obamas' rooms. I re-covered the iconic armchairs that flank the fireplace in leather because it seemed so practical and no-nonsense; it is said that the plants that line the mantel were propagated from Swedish ivy that was given to President Kennedy in the 1960s.

A collection of Chinese export plates with the presidential seal had been displayed on the Oval Office bookshelves for decades. When the president, who had made it clear that he didn't understand this as a design concept, was quoted telling a visiting rear admiral, "I've got to do something about these plates. I'm not really a plate kind of guy," I knew the plates had to go. As I racked my brain for what might be a mindful replacement, I remembered that when I was a schoolkid studying patents, we learned that if you had an invention you wanted to patent, you needed to produce a working model of it — and that patent models were archived at the Smithsonian. I was able to borrow three mid-19th-century models small enough to fit on the shelves: Samuel Morse's telegraph, John A. Peer's gear-cutting machine, and Henry Williams's steamboat paddle wheel. The president loved the concept, as he was famously obsessed with technology and innovation and appreciated the American ingenuity these models represented.

OPPOSITE: On the inset shelves, beautifully bound books share space with Native American pottery, a patent model, and a framed program from the 1963 March on Washington for Jobs and Freedom. ABOVE: Michelle Obama watches as two of Staff Sergeant Clinton Romesha's children choose apples prior to a ceremony at which Sergeant Romesha received the Medal of Honor.

The models shared space on shelves lined with beautifully bound books and four pieces of Native American pottery on loan from the National Museum of the American Indian. The president added a memento with great personal meaning—a framed program and map from the August 1963 March on Washington for Jobs and Freedom, when Dr. Martin Luther King, Jr. delivered his historic "I Have a Dream" speech. In fact, all of the objects and art the president chose for the Oval Office had emotional resonance. I was especially thrilled that we were able to borrow two iconic paintings by Edward Hopper, *Burly Cobb's House, South Truro* and *Cobb's Barns, South Truro*, from the Whitney Museum of American Art, as he was one of the president's favorite artists.

One of our very few disagreements involved his Oval Office curtains. I felt strongly they should be red. Having studied the iconography of various presidents, I realized that many of the important portraits in the White House collection, including those of Washington and Lincoln, featured a swath of red curtain. The color was emblematic of strength of purpose, of heroism; I thought it was important for photographs of President Obama to be framed by this powerful color. The president remained unconvinced, and everyone in his orbit offered a different opinion. Senior advisor Valerie Jarrett suggested white, some people felt they should be blue, others liked gold, but I was firm. They should be red. The president exasperatedly referred to me as "strident" on the subject, but in the end we agreed and he selected a very beautiful barn red woven in a subtle American quilt pattern. The curtains ended up being installed two months after the rest of the office, but they were perfect.

OPPOSITE: Vice President Joe Biden and POTUS head to the Private Dining Room in June 2011 for their weekly lunch. RIGHT: Mementos on the Resolute desk include a gift from former British prime minister Gordon Brown: a penholder crafted from the timbers of the HMS *Gannet*, sister ship to the *Resolute*, from which the desk was carved. The HARD THINGS ARE HARD plaque was given to President Obama by senior advisor David Axelrod during the fight to pass health-care reform. BELOW: President Obama at his desk in October 2016, framed by curtains woven of a barn-red wool in a subtle American-quilt pattern. FOLLOWING PAGES: George Henry Story's portrait of Abraham Lincoln hangs at far left, and the fireplace is flanked by Norman Rockwell's *Statue of Liberty* and a Charles Alston bust of Dr. Martin Luther King, Jr. on the left and Thomas Moran's *The Three Tetons* on the right; Rembrandt Peale's portrait of George Washington hangs above the mantel. Elizabeth Dow hand-printed the striped wallpaper, the sofas by Jonas were upholstered in a Jasper linen velvet, Roman Thomas made the mica-veneered waterfall table, and Christopher Spitzmiller crafted the lamps.

Hard things are hard

PRESIDENT BARACK OBAMA'S
DINING ROOM, HALL, AND STUDY

A private corridor leads from the Oval Office to the president's study and dining room. The Private Dining Room was essentially another working office, an intimate place where the president would have weekly lunches with Vice President Joe Biden, host congressional leaders and visiting dignitaries, and share casual meals with his staff.

We paired a walnut X-base dining table from my Jasper line with a set of Truman-era reproduction Chippendale chairs and had curtains and valances made of a multicolor stripe. I commissioned a patriotic star-pattern carpet for the corridor and dining room in a deep red with gold stars; I used the same motif for the president's study, but woven on a more neutral taupe ground. The walls in both the dining room and study were clad in squares of birch-bark paper, a decision that wasn't merely decorative, but a nod to handcrafted fibers and something that very much reflected Native American and Hawaiian arts and design.

The president's study was a private space, one where he could do research and work quietly during the day. I conceived of it as a retreat, a low-key setting with bark-skin walls and cream linen curtains. His desk was a minimalist design crafted in wood, and I loaned him a comfortable armchair and ottoman for reading. The walls were hung with family photos in narrow black frames, in addition to memorabilia and pieces of art he had collected over time.

These rooms were deeply personal, filled with objects and images with great emotional resonance, including, in the Dining Room, a pair of Muhammad Ali's boxing gloves, autographed "To Barack," displayed in Plexiglas not far from a bust of John F. Kennedy, framed notes from a JFK speech, and a seascape painted by Senator Edward M. Kennedy. And the hall is lined with mementos that include a photo of POTUS with President Nelson Mandela and a framed pen used by President Johnson in 1964 to sign the historic Civil Rights Act.

OPPOSITE: In the Private Dining Room, George P. A. Healy's *The Peacemakers*, an 1868 painting depicting Civil War peace negotiations, is displayed on the far wall; the wool rug was custom made by Scott Group Studio.

MICHAEL S SMITH INTERIORS
ILLUSTRATION / MARK MATUSZAK

PRESIDENT'S DINING ROOM (A)
1600 PENNSYLVANIA AVENUE
WASHINGTON, DC

JUNE 4, 2010

CLOCKWISE, FROM ABOVE: Our palette included deep, rich tones. An early rendering. In May 2012, after a small-business roundtable, President Obama shared sandwiches from a local shop with (*from left*) House Minority Leader Nancy Pelosi, House Speaker John Boehner, Senate Majority Leader Harry Reid, and Senate Minority Leader Mitch McConnell. OPPOSITE: The mirror is 18th-century American; the bust of JFK is by Robert Berks.

OPPOSITE, CLOCKWISE, FROM TOP LEFT: The seascape *Rough Sea at Bailey's Island, Maine* is by Frederick Judd Waugh; the ten-volume series below it, *Abraham Lincoln: A History*, is by John Nicolay and John Hay. *Flag*, a bronze sculpture of the U.S. flag by Jasper Johns, hangs over *Lei O Mano*—a shark's-tooth club mounted and dedicated as the "Favored Weapon of the Royal Hawaiian Kings Bodyguard Proudly Presented to President Barack Obama With Respect From the Men and Women of the Presidential Protective Division." Framed notes for a speech, hand-written by JFK, are displayed above a seascape painted by Senator Ted Kennedy and inscribed, "To Barack, I love your audacity—With great respect and warmest wishes, Ted Kennedy Dec 06," a gift to then–Senator Barack Obama shortly after his second book, *The Audacity of Hope*, was released; we purchased the circa-1857 George III wing chair at auction. Muhammad Ali's autographed boxing gloves. RIGHT: The handmade painted-wood flag was originally displayed in the president's Senate office. Below it to the right are a framed pen and note from Martha Hartke, the widow of a former senator: "With this pen, President Lyndon Johnson signed the historic Civil Rights Act of 1964 and gave it to U.S. Senator Vance Hartke for his support. This gift is given to the Obama family with friendship and ad-miration, and with shared memories of a great struggle." On the left is a photo of President Abraham Lincoln delivering the Gettysburg Address on November 19, 1863. BELOW: Then-senator Obama visiting former president Nelson Mandela in Africa in 2005. BELOW RIGHT: A letter from Natoma Canfield, a self-employed cancer patient who wrote the president in late 2009 to implore him to fight for health-care reform. POTUS said he carried it with him every day until the health-care act was passed; it is framed with the pen he used to sign the 2010 Affordable Care Act into law. The photo below it is of an elderly Theodore Roosevelt leading a stubborn-looking horse up a rocky hill and was given to President Obama by a great-grandson of the late president, who jokingly explained that it was one of Roosevelt's favorite images, as it reminded him of his dealings with Congress.

SAMUEL & SONS
PASSEMENTERIE

OPPOSITE: The walls of the study were clad in the same Caba Company Barkskin that papered the dining room, and the star-motif rug was woven in a warm taupe; matchstick blinds and curtains of a subtle cream striped linen dressed the windows. I paired a classic Eames chair with a modernist lacquered-walnut desk from Twentieth in L.A. and enlarged favorite family photos to display in thin black frames. ABOVE: Not long after the inauguration, carpenter Ed Watson (left) and Bill Allman installed artist Chaz Guest's portrait of Thurgood Marshall, former associate justice of the Supreme Court and the Court's first African American justice, along with representatives from Chicago's DuSable Museum of African American History. The museum originally loaned the portrait to then–Senator Obama, who displayed it in his Capitol Hill office. RIGHT: POTUS, in the early days of his administration, taking a call in his study, which was located down a short hall from the Oval Office and adjacent to the Private Dining Room.

STATE DINING ROOM

Jacqueline Kennedy, during her televised White House tour, described the State Dining Room as having the most architectural unity of any room in the Residence. Theodore Roosevelt's Beaux-Arts renovation had added an elegant classicism—even though the room was paneled in dark oak and displayed hunting trophies mounted on the walls. Reinstalled during the Truman Reconstruction, the paneling was then painted celadon, which Mrs. Kennedy repainted a chalky white, adding touches of gilt as she refined the interior to better reflect its worldly Louis XVI–inflected past.

When I learned in 2011 that the State Dining Room was scheduled for a refresh (it hadn't been updated since 1998), I looked to its classical history for inspiration. We proposed rather simple straight-falling curtains with a swagged valance, similar to those favored by Stéphane Boudin; they were made of an ecru-and-blue striped silk that was woven in Pennsylvania and referenced the Kailua Blue of the Obamas' new porcelain State Service. Scott Group Studio crafted a subtle blue-green rug from my design, which featured an American oak-leaf motif and a wide border ringed with wreaths. They actually made two rugs, as the room got a great deal of wear and tear from public tours and one rug was often out for cleaning.

I was told the room wasn't used frequently for dinners because the Teddy Roosevelt–era chairs were too heavy and cumbersome. (Gilded party chairs were often used for formal events.) After much experimentation, my friend Rachel Kohler, who was then the president of Baker Furniture, Bill Allman, and I landed on a reproduction of a circa-1818 mahogany chair from a suite made by Georgetown furniture maker William King, Jr. for the East Room. I was thrilled: They fit Michelle Obama's mandate that any change must improve the house for the future while mindfully referencing Mrs. Kennedy's Monroe-era ideal for this majestic space.

OPPOSITE: The State Dining Room in 2016, after a three-year refurbishment which included fresh paint in three different hues of white, sumptuous striped-silk curtains, new dining chairs based on James Monroe–era originals, and the installation of a blue-green rug woven with an oak-leaf motif.

MICHAEL S SMITH INTERIORS
ILLUSTRATION / MARK MATUSZAK

STATE DINING ROOM (B)
1600 PENNSYLVANIA AVENUE
WASHINGTON, DC

APRIL 14, 2009

OPPOSITE, FROM TOP: One of several early renderings. We used a warm palette as a counterpoint to the room's chalky white architectural detail; a mahogany chair crafted in Georgetown in 1818 by William King, Jr. inspired the new seating. ABOVE: First Lady Michelle Obama with Bo (*left*) and Sunny in the State Dining Room for a children's holiday event in December 2015; the new curtains were in place, but the oak-leaf rug had yet to be laid. BELOW: The team from J. Edlin Interiors made and installed the curtains and swagged valances, which were sewn of a silk woven in Pennsylvania. The Kailua Blue stripes referenced the blue of the Obamas' porcelain state dinner service. FOLLOWING PAGES: The State Dining Room, the second-largest room in the White House, is used not only for state and formal dinners with tables set for up to 140 guests, but also for official meetings and functions. The eagle console under the mirror, one of three in the room, was designed by Stanford White as part of the 1902 Theodore Roosevelt restoration. Baker Furniture crafted the suite of 34 dining chairs, which were upholstered in a sturdy Brunschwig & Fils horsehair fabric and trimmed with brass nailheads, and Scott Group Studio made a pair of rugs with all-American oak leaves; one could be cleaned while the other was in use.

The President

OLD FAMILY DINING ROOM

Like many good ideas, this project started out small and became big. The long-term concept of expanding inclusivity and diversity in the White House—especially through art and culture—was important and meaningful to President and Mrs. Obama, and our plan to add contemporary art to the State Floor sped from a goal to reality when we recognized the potential of updating the Old Family Dining Room. Located at the west end of the Cross Hall, the room was used primarily for small dinners and working lunches, but also as a staging area for large events and State Dinners because of its proximity to the service elevator to the downstairs kitchen.

It was rife with opportunity: Construction wasn't needed, the art was relatively accessible, and it wouldn't require a great deal of fundraising. In fact, thanks to financial support from the White House Historical Association, we were able to recast the space in record time as well as purchase the White House collection's first work by an African American woman artist, Alma Thomas.

The idea of juxtaposing contemporary paintings into traditional spaces is certainly not novel or new, but it was clearly groundbreaking for the State Floor. A Robert Rauschenberg work became the cornerstone for the room's transformation, and then the Josef and Anni Albers Foundation serendipitously gave us two Albers paintings and funding to make a carpet based on an Anni Albers weaving. The existing furnishings included a Kennedy-era mahogany dining table with a mix of antique and reproduction chairs and an early 19th-century chest of drawers and sideboard; the marble mantel was highly ornamented. I hung simple curtains of a red linen-silk, creating a very spare 18th-century background designed to make the art more prominent.

OPPOSITE: A porcelain place setting from the Obama State Service, which was made by Pickard China; the napkin is embroidered with the presidential coat of arms. The ornate marble mantel, purchased in France from Maison Jansen, dates from the Kennedy restoration.

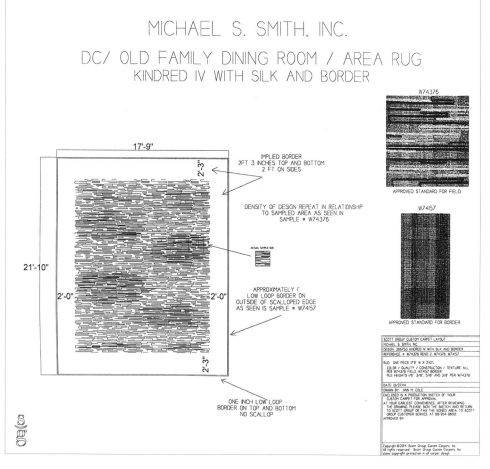

ABOVE: Because of its proximity to the pantry and downstairs kitchen, the Old Family Dining Room continues to serve as the kitchen staff's staging area for large events and State Dinners. LEFT: A production drawing by Scott Group Studio for the wool-and-silk rug they made based on a weaving by artist Anni Albers. OPPOSITE: In April 2016, President and Mrs. Obama hosted their annual Passover Seder for friends and staff. FOLLOWING PAGES: Our new version of the Old Family Dining Room featured pale gray walls and red linen-silk curtains with simple tiebacks; the circa-1800 mahogany dining table is surrounded by antique and reproduction chairs. The focus of the room was the art—beginning with the rug, which was adapted from *Black, White, and Gray,* an Anni Albers pictorial weaving. Robert Rauschenberg's *Early Bloomer [Anagram (a Pun)]* is displayed above an 1820 mahogany sideboard and a silver coffee and tea service made for the U.S. pavilion at the 1939 New York World's Fair. *Resurrection,* a painting by Alma Thomas, was the first work by an African American woman purchased for the White House collection; it hangs over an early 19th-century chest of drawers. Out of view are two works by Josef Albers, *Study for Homage to the Square: Asking* and *Homage to the Square.*

This was in line with the Obamas' mindset of always honoring what was beautiful and historic while adding to and improving whatever was already in place. In February 2015, Michelle Obama opened the room to the public on the official White House tour for the first time ever, enabling its more than one million annual visitors to experience the vitality and creativity of the space for themselves.

The dining room was a key part of the Obama legacy, and events held there assumed perhaps an even greater meaning. Valerie Jarrett, the president's senior advisor, told me about one in particular, the Obamas' annual Passover Seder, a ritual that started on the campaign trail in April 2008. After a full day of rallies, then–Senator Obama wanted to make sure the young staffers—many of whom had never been away for Passover before—had a traditional Seder. At the end of the evening, he promised, "If I win, next year in the White House." For the next eight years, he invited the guests from that first Seder to share Passover dinner in the Old Family Dining Room. With each passing year, some married and had children, and others brought their moms or dads. Valerie said, "Believe me, there were people clamoring to be at that Seder!"

Valerie told me that the president wanted to thank those who were with him in Pennsylvania for that first Passover when no one really believed this was possible and who gave up so much of their family life for the cause. "This is just one example," she said, "of how President Obama invited people here to thank them and to let their families know—and feel—that they were part of this journey too."

7   THE DIPLOMACY OF ART

As soon as First Lady Michelle Obama's reinvention of the Old Family Dining Room was completed in early 2015, she turned to her friend Jenna Bush Hager, a *Today* show correspondent and former first daughter, to help her reveal its celebration of modern art and design to the public. During the interview, she explained to Jenna how mindful her decisions had been: "You feel a really huge responsibility to make sure that the changes reflect the values of the house, that they reflect the values of the country."

Mindfulness defined the Obamas' all-embracing focus on American art and culture right from the start, a focus that evolved and grew throughout the president's two terms and formed a significant part of the Obama administration's White House legacy. My role was as art advisor in terms of the interiors, and in the weeks prior to the inauguration, to re-

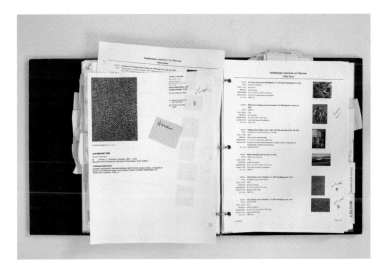

search potential art loans I met with museum curators, directors, and board chairs and spent hours on my laptop searching museum collections for treasures that were in storage. (We knew to request only art not on display, so the public would not be deprived in any way.) I envisioned a group of works assembled from a range of the nation's cultural institutions that would not only represent a true cross section of the best of American art, but also reflect the voices of the different constituencies that brought the Obamas to the White House—certainly women, as well as other social, racial, and ethnic minorities, especially the African American community and Latino Americans.

OPPOSITE: Michelle Obama with Jenna Bush Hager at the opening of the Old Family Dining Room on February 10, 2015, when it was added to the public tours as a showcase for contemporary art. ABOVE: I compiled binders of potential museum loans for the president and first lady to consider; they would flag and initial works that they liked best.

Unfortunately, my plans were derailed by both cost and logistics when I learned that I had been misinformed. While the White House can borrow art—and museums are usually eager to lend—there are no budget funds allocated for shipping and insurance, which are two of the major costs in terms of loans and producing exhibitions. Curators know this; I didn't.

However, I soon discovered that the Smithsonian has an overriding umbrella insurance policy that would cover any loans to the White House, amounting to enormous savings. The federal museums and their curators truly became our saviors—especially National Gallery of Art curators Molly Donovan and Harry Cooper with then-museum director Rusty Powell, and Hirshhorn Museum and Sculpture Garden curator Evelyn Hankins and Kerry Brougher, at the time the museum's acting director. They were invaluable partners on this project; everyone was excited to help communicate the cultural mindset of the new administration, and they worked with me to find striking contemporary American works, many by artists who would never have appeared in the White House before.

> "We had never been asked to install works on an Inauguration Day, but Michael made it a huge priority. The White House loan was the largest extended to a government agency during the Obama administration. Also, they were primarily modern and contemporary works, which was a major shift. Michael reshaped the whole concept of art in the White House. By bringing in contemporary works, he celebrated artists – living artists and their artwork – and really brought the conversation forward. He made that historic building feel very fresh and relevant. The trajectory of the visibility of artists also changed as the Obamas focused on the inclusiveness of all kinds of artists from different backgrounds. They looked carefully at how to represent the face of the nation – it was really important in that moment. This was a seismic shift in my mind.
>
> President and Mrs. Obama showed leadership in their decisions about the art they chose to display. The Obama administration's strong embrace of modern and contemporary works in the private residence signaled an enormous change and set a powerful example. It was clearly the highest profile imaginable."

> – *Molly Donovan, curator of contemporary art at the National Gallery of Art*

On my first walk-through of the State Floor, I had realized that much of the White House collection was based on historic portraiture, which was appropriate and looked beautiful in all the State Rooms—the Blue Room, Green Room, and Red Room, culminating with the Lincoln portrait in the State Dining Room and George Washington's life-size portrait in the East Room. These are some of the most exquisite spaces I've ever been in. But upstairs in the private quarters, historic portraits seemed static and dark, even a bit haunting, and the addition of contemporary paintings would infuse the Obamas' new home with a fresh spirit and vitality.

I initially compiled a selection of options by culling from the museum websites, searching

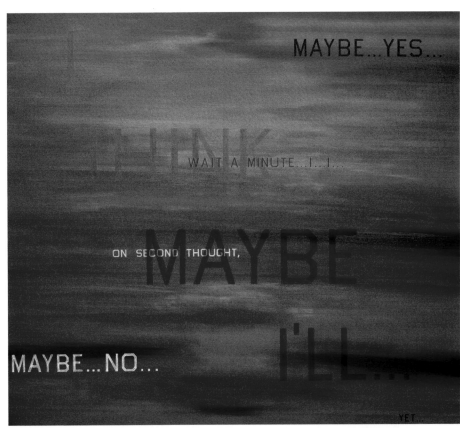

CLOCKWISE, FROM ABOVE: President Obama with Secretary of State Hillary Clinton in the Blue Room, beneath George P. A. Healy's portrait of President John Tyler. Ed Ruscha's painting *I Think I'll...* was borrowed from the National Gallery. Staffers installing Shepard Fairey's iconic campaign-poster portrait of Barack Obama at the National Portrait Gallery in January 2009.

CLOCKWISE, FROM FAR LEFT: The president is drawn to text-based art and admired Glenn Ligon's work; he acquired two of the artist's lithographs, which we hung in the Billiard Room. We borrowed Ligon's *Black Like Me #2* from the Hirshhorn Museum to install in the Family Sitting Room. When the Norman Rockwell Museum loaned Rockwell's *The Problem We All Live With* to the White House for a short-term exhibition in the West Wing, President Obama invited civil-rights icon Ruby Bridges, the young girl portrayed in the painting, to view it displayed outside the Oval Office. OPPOSITE: The president in February 2014 with two works by Edward Hopper, one of his favorite artists; the paintings were loaned by the Whitney Museum to hang in the Oval Office.

for key works that were marked as not being on display. I chose carefully, avoiding pieces that had the potential to be requested for external exhibitions. I also kept in mind that though we were allowed to borrow the work of living artists, there was a standing rule that pieces could not be purchased for the White House collection — except by special commission — to avoid controversy regarding price and value. I thought there were definite gaps in the collection — for instance, there were no abstract works — which offered the opportunity for the administration to recommend choices that would add greater relevancy and diversity to the holdings.

I organized binders for the president and first lady to review, and they each flagged and initialed works they liked that were worthy of a follow-up. This was truly liberating for me, as consulting on art purchases has clearly been a part of my practice for decades, and here we were solely concerned with loans — price and perceived value were not major considerations. Decisions were ultimately based on historic reference, the diversity of the artists, the beauty of the work — in truth, so many elements — but for once, works of great and modest value were on equal footing.

The first lady was mainly focused on the overall vision of our mission, and I discovered works by artists I was unfamiliar with, such as Alma Thomas, an African American former schoolteacher who didn't turn to painting full-time until she was 60 years old. President Obama, however, has had a long association with art and artists, perhaps best exemplified by Shepard Fairey's iconic *Hope* poster that was so emblematic of the 2008 campaign that the National Portrait Gallery put it on display just prior to the first Obama inauguration. Our art selections also reflected primarily on the president — when we installed Ed Ruscha's cryptic *I Think I'll...* canvas in the Center Hall, pundits were quick to voice that it symbolized his indecision, an allegation that ignored both fact and reason. And later, artist Rob Pruitt famously documented the administration in his series *The Obama Paintings* — painting one two-foot-square canvas each of Barack Obama's 2,922 days in office.

The Obamas were celebrated for the art that we put on display — including masterful works by Hans Hofmann, Susan Rothenberg, Barnett Newman, Robert Rauschenberg, Sam Francis, Josef Albers, Jacob Lawrence, Mark Rothko, Pat Steir, Glenn Ligon, Sean Scully, William H. Johnson, Louise Nevelson, and Robert Mangold — and derided for not featuring enough female artists and not one Latino American. To be honest, being limited to the national museums was an issue, as there were fewer works from which to choose. I was also disappointed to not be able to showcase works by groundbreaking artists such as Lorna Simpson, Mark Bradford, and Mickalene Thomas; their works remain largely in private collections, and those held by museums were not yet plentiful enough to be sent out on loan.

There was a learning curve: Bill Allman explained why White House art often looks as if it is hung too high (soaring ceilings, and to protect them from floral arrangements and clumsy guests). And though I relentlessly tried to make *Two Maps*, an extraordinary Jasper Johns painting, work in the Oval Office, an overscale canvas isn't meant to hang on a curved wall.

> "I was excited to be included in anything that had to do with the Obamas. He was a remarkable president and they had an important cultural presence. At Michelle Obama's reception to celebrate American art and artists, there were people of all ages and genders and races represented. It was thrilling to see that in the White House."
>
> — *Pat Steir, artist*

However, if the 2015 opening of the Old Family Dining Room as a gallery for contemporary art represented the zenith of our yearslong project, the most inspiring and emotional

day for me was nearly two years prior, when Michelle Obama hosted a reception in recognition of American art and in honor of the White House Historical Association's unwavering support. The State Dining Room overflowed with art-world luminaries, from collectors to museum curators to the artists themselves, both emerging talents and art icons such as Pat Steir, Kerry James Marshall, Catherine Opie, and Julie Mehretu. Most had never before been invited to the White House, and many were overcome with pride; I was filled with joy. Mrs. Obama spoke of her admiration for art and artists and how thrilled she was to announce the gift of a Robert Rauschenberg painting and two Josef Albers works to the collection. This was a historic moment in the Obama legacy — a celebration of art, culture, diversity, and inclusiveness — a moment shared with some of the greatest talents of our time.

OPPOSITE: My friends Glenn Ligon and Thelma Golden, the director of the Studio Museum in Harlem, with me at the opening of New York City's Renzo Piano–designed Whitney Museum of American Art. CLOCKWISE, FROM TOP LEFT: The first lady at an East Room reception in June 2013 to celebrate the gift of works by Robert Rauschen- berg and Josef Albers to the permanent White House collection. Mrs. Obama was asked to help dedicate the new Whitney Museum in April 2015. Artist Rob Pruitt's 2,922 indi- vidual two-foot-square paintings on display at the Stony Island Arts Bank on Chicago's South Side; Pruitt created them as a daily documentation of the Obama administration.

8   A CULTURE OF INCLUSION

It was apparent early on that President and Mrs. Obama's welcoming, open-minded style would permeate every aspect of their White House life. The Residence has long been known as the People's House, a concept they fervently embraced and a term they used regularly throughout their administration. Very much conscious of the gravity of the roles they had taken on, the Obamas had made it a priority to stay connected with former first families and appreciated their advice regarding their respective experiences—especially as the president and first lady were laser-focused on creating as normal a life as possible for their daughters. Mrs. Obama felt the house should always be open to former first families and regularly invited them. But it was also a time to put their own imprint not only on this groundbreaking presidency, but on the White House and its long-standing traditions.

Most institutions are highly resistant to change, and there was a strong sense in America that if you broke tradition, the dignity of the presidency itself was being assaulted. President and Mrs. Obama never accepted that notion; being conventional wasn't their style, and they recognized their ability to bridge the formality of the building with relevance and accessibility for all. Perhaps because they had young children, they were keenly aware that they needed to create events where guests felt comfortable and felt that they belonged. From the annual Easter Egg Roll to elegant State Dinners, poetry jams, Kennedy Center Honors celebrations, hip-hop dances, and Girl Scout sleepovers on the South Lawn, President and Mrs. Obama welcomed all ages and strata of society to the People's House—including a remarkably diverse group of artists, creative talents, scientists, and thought leaders. I felt their mission was to make their presidency emblematic of American democracy itself.

Their first formal event, the annual Governors' Ball, always takes place mid-February. Every state governor is invited, and a range of meetings are held throughout the next

OPPOSITE: At the February 2009 Governors' Ball, the first formal event of the Obama administration, President and Mrs. Obama dance in the East Room to the music of the band Earth, Wind & Fire.

day. But before all the seriously partisan politics with stridently right- and left-wing governors got in full swing that first year, Mrs. Obama wanted to make the opening night's gala exciting, memorable, and fun.

> *"The Governors' Ball is the first formal event hosted by the president and first lady. Honoring the longtime tradition of entertainment following the dinner, Mrs. Obama asked me, 'Wouldn't it be spectacular to have a really fun dance party?' Enter Earth, Wind & Fire! The evening ended well into the night with many of the nation's governors dancing out of the East Room in a conga line."*

> **—Desirée Rogers, former White House social secretary**

In her memoir, *Becoming*, Michelle Obama recalls thinking that her White House life could be forward leaning while still respecting tradition. Her goal was to make the White House feel more open, welcoming, and accessible to all Americans. And as focused as the first lady would be on the scores of nearly daily receptions and events the Obamas hosted—for which she relied heavily on her White House executive chef Cristeta Comerford and social secretaries, who had included Desirée Rogers, Julianna Smoot, Jeremy Bernard, and Deesha Dyer and their teams—I think her favorite event was always the Kids' State Dinner. The party was an offshoot of Mrs. Obama's Let's Move! campaign, launched in early 2010

OPPOSITE: On Halloween 2015, the president and first lady react as a young trick-or-treater dressed as the pope pulls up in a popemobile. The White House was decorated for Halloween every year, and the Obamas welcomed local children and the children of military families with baskets of treats outside the South Portico. ABOVE: The East Room set up for the fourth annual Kids' State Dinner, which was held on July 10, 2015; guests, aged 8 to 12 years old, had won a contest challenging them to create an original recipe that was healthy, affordable, and delicious. Recipes were later compiled in a cookbook published by the WHHA—I'm personally obsessed with the Indian Tacos from the state of Wyoming. RIGHT: Following the East Room unveiling of the official portraits of President George W. Bush and First Lady Laura Bush in May 2012, the Obamas hosted a luncheon in the Red Room for members of the Bush family.

CLOCKWISE, FROM ABOVE: A trio of State Dinners created by event designer Bryan Rafanelli: The Obamas hosted an idyllic State Dinner in the Rose Garden in honor of German Chancellor Angela Merkel and her husband, Dr. Joachim Sauer, on June 7, 2011. Mary J. Blige performs in a tent on the South Lawn during the State Dinner in honor of President François Hollande of France on February 11, 2014. Our new Obama State Service porcelain table settings were featured at the April 28, 2015, State Dinner in honor of Japanese Prime Minister Shinzo Abe and his wife, Akie.

to inspire kids to exercise and eat well, and her Healthy Lunchtime Challenge, a contest for children to create recipes for healthy, affordable, and tasty meals. In August 2012, the 56 contest winners and a parent or guardian were invited to the first annual Kids' State Dinner, which was really a super-fun lunch for kids between the ages 8 and 12 from all 50 states, five U.S. territories, and the District of Columbia. The East Room was decked out with tables set with towering topiaries of vegetables and fruit, and the children dined on the White House china. The WHHA compiled a selection of recipes in an amazing cookbook, whose sales benefit White House programs.

"What I love about Mrs. Obama is that for an event like a State Dinner, she really wanted a narrative. She wanted it to connect to a story, and she needed it to have a purpose. The symbolism was so critical; she didn't just want it to be pretty. An Obama State Dinner mindfully represented the country we were honoring while it celebrated the very best of America. And even though we invented something completely different each time, creativity wasn't what mattered most; making a real connection was her primary goal. The first lady understood the importance of design and diplomacy, and she was comfortable making bold choices; she wanted to make each event special for every person there.

There are so many official rules regarding the White House — it's a historic house as well as a museum — but we built up trust with the curators and were able to push the envelope to create some exciting installations, especially during the holidays. We could hang things on the sconces, drape garlands over massive mirrors, and wedge towering stacks of presents in between the columns. One year we hung the East Colonnade with 3,000 snowflakes that local schoolkids had made and written their holiday wishes on; another year the hall was transformed with thousands of ribbon streamers in electric colors. And we always recycled and reinvented as much as we could from previous holidays.

I'm honored to have been involved in 25 events at the White House — from seven State Dinners to the Governors' Ball, Kids' State Dinners, and holiday parties. I saw the extraordinary respect that everyone had for the building. The Obamas were such a modern family, and everything they did was well considered and reflected the present — in design, in the way they entertained, and in how they treated people. They breathed new life into the White House."

— Bryan Rafanelli, event designer

In addition to countless official and cultural events, President and Mrs. Obama staged 13 State Dinners over eight years (by comparison, the George W. Bushes also hosted 13, the Clintons clocked in at 29, and the Reagans organized a whopping 52 State Visits). Because of their scale and logistics, the galas, which are funded by the State Department, often require months of advance work. FLOTUS sometimes asked me to review the setup or weigh in on the ancillary events that took place during a State Visit, but professional event designers — including the celebrated firms of both David Monn and Bryan Rafanelli — were always engaged to handle the conception and production. There was constant buzz and excitement surrounding the galas—what would the room look like? What was the special menu being served? Would the first lady wear a gown by a designer from the country that was being honored? I was particularly thrilled to have experienced the magic firsthand as a guest at the State Dinners in honor of French President François Hollande in 2014 and for Italian Prime Minister Matteo Renzi two years later.

The president and first lady had mentioned to me how much they enjoyed spending time on the Truman Balcony—during receptions held in the adjacent Yellow Oval Room, and also at the end of the day, as it was the only relatively private place they could sit outside. I decorated the space as an outdoor living room, grouping glass hurricane candleholders to provide soft lighting in the evening. After receiving a series of calls in L.A. requesting

replacements, I finally asked what was going on. Bill Allman told me that they kept shattering. On my next visit I saw that they had imploded, with the glass crushed in. We figured out it had something to do with the aerodynamic force of Marine One taking off and landing so close to the Truman Balcony; sometimes the chair cushions would end up

on the lawn as well. I replaced the glass hurricanes with Plexiglas ones. In truth, the first time I saw the president land, I was spellbound; that helicopter is like a giant insect—or spaceship—hovering just yards away. The juxtaposition of this historic house and the high-tech helicopter was truly surreal.

One of my most patriotic experiences with the Obama family was being invited to their Fourth of July celebration the summer we lived in Washington for James's ambassadorship training before we left for Spain. There was a giant picnic on the lawn for military families, and we watched the fireworks from the roof terrace off of the Solarium. It was Malia's birthday, and the girls were super excited: There was incredible music, the sky was bursting with amazing fireworks, and the Washington Monument was smack in front of us. We were captivated.

President and Mrs. Obama created so many thrilling experiences—especially the spectacular holiday decorations and events they produced year after year, conjuring joy and magic even during difficult times, and the extraordinary talents they invited to perform at the White House. They cared deeply about integrity, quality, and relevance as they welcomed

OPPOSITE: On May 12, 2009, at a special White House event, Lin-Manuel Miranda performed a song from an early iteration of what would become *Hamilton*. ABOVE: President and Mrs. Obama and their daughter Malia (*center*) watch Fourth of July fireworks in 2014; the holiday is also Malia's birthday. One of the most patriotic experiences from my years working with the Obamas was watching the fireworks with their family from the White House roof. BELOW: Marine One as it departs from the South Lawn, remarkably close to the Truman Balcony. LEFT: The first lady chats with United Kingdom Prime Minister David Cameron and his wife, Samantha, on the Truman Balcony during a reception on March 14, 2012. I decorated the balcony, which is adjacent to the Yellow Oval Room, both for entertaining and as a relatively private place for the family to relax.

CLOCKWISE, FROM TOP LEFT: My longtime collaborator Mark Matuszak created the Obamas' 2011 holiday card, which featured family dog Bo in front of the Library fireplace; I loved the idea that after all of the renderings of new rooms he created for the Obamas, he painted a space that had been so beautifully redone by the Bushes. In December 2016, the East Colonnade was lined with thousands of satin-ribbon streamers in a myriad of colors. This hall overlooks the Jacqueline Kennedy Garden on the left, which is usually decorated as well; the Family Theater, located through a door on the right, serves as the coat-check room for large events. White House pastry chef Susie Morrison constructs a meticulously detailed gingerbread version of the Residence in the China Room on November 29, 2010. Massive replicas of Obama pets Bo and Sunny, crafted of 25,000 yarn pom-poms, greeted holiday guests during the 2016 holiday season, which was the Obama family's last Christmas in the White House. OPPOSITE: Every year, there is an army of White House Christmas trees (there were 67 trees in 2016) that are decorated with the assistance of scores of volunteers; the largest tree is installed in the center of the Blue Room, where the chandelier is always removed in order to accommodate the height of the tree. This stately 2009 tree stood 18 feet tall and nearly 13 feet wide.

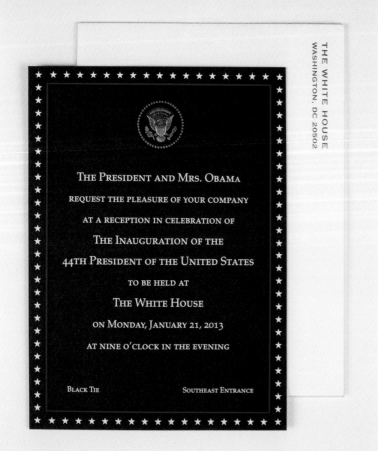

THE WHITE HOUSE
WASHINGTON, DC 20502

THE PRESIDENT AND MRS. OBAMA

REQUEST THE PLEASURE OF YOUR COMPANY

AT A RECEPTION IN CELEBRATION OF

THE INAUGURATION OF THE

44TH PRESIDENT OF THE UNITED STATES

TO BE HELD AT

THE WHITE HOUSE

ON MONDAY, JANUARY 21, 2013

AT NINE O'CLOCK IN THE EVENING

BLACK TIE   SOUTHEAST ENTRANCE

ABOVE: Mindful of the nation's ongoing economic crisis, President Obama's 2013 inauguration was designed to be more low-key than his historic Inauguration Day four years prior. Because January 20 fell on a Sunday that year, he was officially sworn in by Chief Justice John Roberts in the White House Blue Room with the first lady and daughters Malia and Sasha in attendance, the day before a reported one million people attended the public inaugural ceremony at the Capitol. Though there were several high-profile celebrations that evening, the president and first lady only attended the two official inaugural balls (they danced at ten galas in 2009, though some 121 unofficial balls were held). The Obamas were known for throwing incredible White House gatherings with some of the most iconic musical artists of our time, often followed by a favorite DJ like DJ Cassidy—and the private after-party the president and first lady hosted at 9 P.M. the evening of the inauguration was one of the most joyful experiences of my entire life. While researching White House photos of the event, we happened to find this one, picturing James dancing with me next to President and Mrs. Obama. I think then–House Minority Leader Nancy Pelosi is just out of the frame, as I remember that she and I were dancing to Beyoncé's "Single Ladies," which at the time was beyond crazy, not to mention wildly fun. LEFT: The invitation to the Obamas' private 2013 Inaugural Ball after-party at the White House.

some of the most compelling singers and musicians in the country, never failing to respect the legacy of previous historic performances. I was there the night Lin-Manuel Miranda previewed an astounding piece from what would become the transformational Broadway blockbuster *Hamilton*, as well as other amazing evenings filled with music and song. Special events included everything from Gershwin to Motown, Broadway to a celebration of Latin music, the finest classical music to hip-hop, Janelle Monáe to Aretha Franklin, and Yo-Yo Ma to Bruce Springsteen. You can find the performance videos on the archived Obama White House website; they're fascinating to watch.

But for me, the most unforgettable night was the after-party on the night of the 2013 inauguration. The election was clear-cut, and there would now be the opportunity to complete the goals formed during the first four years without the distraction of a campaign. Second-term inaugurations are always less dramatic, and after attending the two official balls, the Obamas planned an early celebration for friends and family that turned out to be a blowout dance party.

> *"One late night in the East Room, I danced under an enormous portrait of George Washington while Prince performed for a hundred or so of the Obamas' guests. The music was thumping, the crowd was jumping — literally — '1999' or 'Purple Rain' or something equally amazing was happening, and it felt like we were all happier than we'd ever been, like even George Washington was dancing a little bit. Then, spontaneously, Stevie Wonder decided that he, too, wanted to play. So there I stood, an arm's distance away, and watched as Prince played backup for Stevie Wonder. The two of them together sounded... well, like Stevie Wonder and Prince together. I stood and stared. I am thinking, Who would believe this was possible? And at just that point, Prince looked up and his eyes locked with mine. He cocked his head, eyes filled with joy, and mouthed, 'Can you believe this?' He couldn't believe it was possible either. Prince was having one of these moments in this White House, too. So much of my experience in the Obama-era White House was 'Who would believe this was possible?' Most of the moments I had with the people, with the era, with the place itself were moments bigger than I had ever dreamed. Moments bigger than I could ever make up to write for my TV shows. And I could make up a lot. The imprint it left on me is specific and indelible. If you watch any of my shows, it left an imprint on you as well."*

> *— Shonda Rhimes, screenwriter, television producer, author*

The tension of the election and uncertainty of its outcome were gone, and there was a palpable sense of relief. Then, what had started off as a cool, elegant cocktail reception was transformed once the performances started. Michelle Obama stood up and started dancing, and there was an immediate rush of joy and energy at this exciting moment in history. The party lasted well into the morning hours, capped by the president and Usher having a Gangnam-style dance-off. I can't recall who won, but Prince clearly said it best: "Can you believe this?"

Color Swatches and Fabric Samples from the OVAL OFFICE Makeover

sage

walnut

wingnut

wonk

mochachino

grey-poupon

creme brulee

taupey changey

too beige to fail

drab

no drama

muslin
(that's muslin, with an **N**)

reddish

radish

nebbish

sand

sandtrap

putting green

tarp green

eggshell

salmonella

9   PROJECTS AND PROGRESS

In September 2010, I was reading a copy of *The New Yorker* on a flight home to L.A. and came across a drawing by cartoonist Barry Blitt that riffed on the color palette of our Oval Office redecoration. The update had just been released to the public and attracted some attention. It was funny—"muslin (that's musli<u>n</u>, with an <u>N</u>)"—but also sort of crazy. I never imagined that my work might be fodder for a *New Yorker* cartoon, even though from the start I had been aware that my responsibilities at the White House might hold a greater significance than decorating. My role was to create a beautifully designed envelope within which the first family could navigate their highly demanding lives, find comfort, and thrive, but I also needed to ensure that the work was relevant, my narrative was appropriate, and the optics were unfailingly correct.

> *"Michael was very invested in the history of the building, and he was very intentional. He wasn't just bringing in pieces that he thought the Obamas would like. He understood the gravity and uniqueness of his position and took it very seriously. He thought through everything down to the last detail, and he did his homework—whether it was his mindfulness about the crafting of the Oval Office rug or always providing the backstory to a piece of art and the artist who made it."*
>
> *— Melissa Winter, former deputy chief of staff to First Lady Michelle Obama*

People always seem surprised to learn that the White House design project is one that never truly ends until the first family moves out after four or eight years. Once the primary decoration is completed, there are constant small updates, maintenance, and renovation projects, as well as the ongoing work overseen by the offices of the curator and chief usher—including chairs that need reupholstering and table lamps that break. But there were weightier issues that I wanted to tackle as well, including becoming very involved with the reelection campaign and working to support the Obama Victory Fund.

As the 2012 campaign ramped up, James and I cohosted a variety of events with other

OPPOSITE: It was a fun surprise to discover cartoonist Barry Blitt's humorous drawing of the Oval Office color palette in *The New Yorker*, which was published in the September 13, 2010, issue, just after our redesign of the space was revealed.

supporters at various venues in L.A. and New York, and we agreed to stage an upcoming event for President Obama at our New York apartment. In truth, we had never hosted a political fundraiser before. Little did we know, it would spark our deep competitiveness to succeed, not just within the campaign world at large, but even with each other.

Our event was planned as a dessert reception on March 1; it was one of a few consecutive fundraisers at which the president would appear and make brief remarks. A wide range of friends committed to attend, and we cleared all but essential furniture from our apartment into storage for the night. The Secret Service did a thorough sweep, and after they insisted that we close the curtains at every window for security (we live in a penthouse with four exposures and wraparound terraces), I decided to tent the back terrace and rent panels of faux boxwood that were placed outside all the windows as a screen.

> *"So let me start off by thanking Michael and James. They could not be better friends. And for them to open up their home to us just means so much. It is a special treat for me because, as some of you know, Michael has been redesigning the White House. And he has some strong opinions. [Laughter] And sometimes doesn't always agree with my taste. And so it is good to come to his house and critique it. I don't know about this whole thing right here. [Laughter] Actually, he has done a remarkable job, despite me. So I'm grateful to him."*

> *— President Barack Obama, transcript of remarks at a March 1, 2012, campaign fundraiser*

Traffic in our neighborhood came to a standstill after nearby streets were blocked — and as excited as our neighbors were that the president would be in our building, they were surely cursing us. But we had a great turnout, and in addition to POTUS coolly name-checking John Legend in the crowd — announcing that because the music star was present, he wouldn't be singing — the president took the opportunity to tease me about my taste, jokingly questioning the look of the antiqued-mirror wall behind him.

OPPOSITE, FROM TOP: President Obama makes remarks on March 1, 2012, at an Obama Victory Fund reception that James and I hosted at our New York apartment. A few months later, at our house in L.A., I introduced FLOTUS at another campaign fundraiser. ABOVE: On June 26, 2015, the Obamas had the White House lit in rainbow colors to celebrate the Supreme Court ruling in support of same-sex marriage.

CLOCKWISE, FROM TOP: The president and first lady received countless gifts over the course of their eight years in office (they were unable to keep most personal gifts due to ethics protocol), and I would sometimes receive calls for suggestions of where to place certain objects in the Residence; here, POTUS was presented with a rocking chair from the NCAA champion University of Connecticut Huskies women's basketball team in May 2016. I was also asked to suggest potential presents the Obamas might give to others—either as personal thank-yous or as official State gifts; we often looked to American artisans for options, including artist Nancy Lorenz, who crafts exquisite silver-leafed boxes drizzled with gold resin. For my 50th birthday, President Obama gave me a set of beautiful framed prints from the National Archives of original renderings of historic decorative objects designed for use in the White House, which I love.

I have to admit, it was strange having the president at our apartment, despite his charisma and ease. It was two worlds interconnecting, a bit like seeing your schoolteacher at the grocery store. Undeterred, just a few months later James and I hosted a similar campaign reception with Mrs. Obama at our L.A. house and saw her completely captivate the hundreds of guests who stood starstruck on the lawn before her. She was warm, funny, and natural; she spoke with grace and conviction, words that were evocative of the fundamental values held by us all. Though I had heard her speak many times before, this speech gave me a hint of the monumental power of her persona. Every one of us was enchanted, and her presence served as a touchstone, motivating many other people who were there that evening to then host their own fundraisers over the months leading to the election.

We were also extremely supportive of our friends Michele and Rob Reiner and Chad Griffin, who were hugely instrumental in overturning California's discriminatory Prop 8 legislation, setting the stage for marriage equality for all. We set up residence in Europe for James's post as ambassador to Spain and Andorra not long after the law was repealed in 2013. James was the first openly gay ambassador to be dispatched to a major European country — likely because Spain had approved same-sex marriage nearly a decade earlier, in 2005. And though we were in Spain in June 2015, when the Supreme Court ruled in favor of marriage equality, those were exciting moments for all and something particularly personal for us. We were overjoyed when the White House was illuminated in the colors of the rainbow.

As I started to take on other design-related projects at the White House, I would sometimes receive calls regarding where in the Residence the Obamas might want to place an official gift they had received — they were given countless presents throughout their two terms, though due to ethics protocol, most personal gifts had to be gracefully returned and significant gifts from foreign leaders were sent off to the National Archives. The Obamas were always very precise regarding presidential rules and regulations.

I would also advise on presents for them to give — both as diplomatic gifts through the State Department and even ideas for personal thank-yous, as it was inconceivable for FLOTUS to shop without causing a riot. Both the president and first lady were drawn to pieces by American artisans, and I sourced objects like handblown-glass vases and bowls by Caleb Simon and Carmen Salazar in California and exquisite boxes by New York–based artist Nancy Lorenz. We also suggested beautiful, less precious items like blankets and throws handmade in Maine or Kentucky. Among the most sought-after gifts was White House honey from the Kitchen Garden beehives, and we designed honey bottles for special presentations, very conscious of the impact of even a small token if it was given by the Obamas.

The Obama State Service porcelain, which Bill Allman and I developed in collaboration with Andrew Pickard Morgan of Pickard China in Illinois, was an important project that fascinated me because of the Obamas' reputation for elegant entertaining and the role that the china would play in their presidential legacy. The first lady's directive was clear: to create a fresh, modern design that referenced the past, would coordinate well with china from prior administrations, and resolve kitchen- and serving-staff concerns regarding food temperature and ease of service. (White House china must withstand a constant beating as staff serve and remove place settings from tightly seated tables within strict time constraints.) After careful deliberation with Bill, Andy, and Mrs. Obama, we created a color called Kailua Blue, named for the waters of the president's home state of Hawaii, which is used as a fluted band rimmed in gold on many of the pieces; the presidential coat of arms appears on the dessert and service plates, and the dinner plate and a new tureen shape reference a James Madison–era porcelain pattern. Arriving just in time for the April 2015 Japan State Dinner, our order for 320 11-piece place settings, funded by the WHHA, received a glowing response.

In 2009, Mrs. Obama came to the White House with a lineup of key policy initiatives, and while still adjusting her family to their new home, she set to work to achieve her mission.

MICHAEL S SMITH INTERIORS
ILLUSTRATION / MARK MATUSZAK

WHITE HOUSE DISHES
1600 PENNSYLVANIA AVENUE
WASHINGTON, DC

APRIL 18, 2012

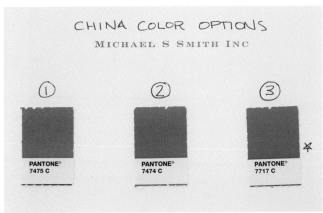

CHINA COLOR OPTIONS
MICHAEL S SMITH INC

① PANTONE 7475 C ② PANTONE 7474 C ③ PANTONE 7717 C

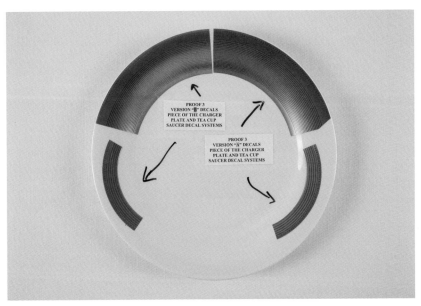

PROOF 3
VERSION "B" DECALS
PIECE OF THE CHARGER
PLATE AND TEA CUP
SAUCER DECAL SYSTEMS

PROOF 3
VERSION "A" DECALS
PIECE OF THE CHARGER
PLATE AND TEA CUP
SAUCER DECAL SYSTEMS

OPPOSITE: Our rendering for the proposed Obama china. CLOCKWISE, FROM TOP LEFT: The press frenzy on April 27, 2015, when the new porcelain was revealed at the Japan State Dinner preview. Color chips I mixed for early Kailua Blue border ideas. Select designs from the 11-piece State Service place settings, which were made by Pickard China. Mrs. Obama examines a porcelain teacup at the china preview. A plate with glaze tests for review.

CLOCKWISE, FROM ABOVE: Sam Kass speaking about nutrition at the 2014 Kids' State Dinner; formerly the Obama family's chef, Sam became a White House senior food policy advisor and the executive director of Let's Move!, the first lady's program to counteract childhood obesity. In the White House Kitchen Garden, FLOTUS harvests vegetables with Sam Kass and local students; the first lady planted the Kitchen Garden in April 2009, with the goal for it to serve as a "learning garden," a way to teach children about the food cycle and eating healthfully. The 2,800-square-foot garden now produces 2,000 pounds of food for the first family, White House guests, and local Washington, D.C., organizations feeding those in need. Mrs. Obama tours the Kitchen Garden with Queen Letizia of Spain on her September 2015 visit to the White House; I was off camera, poised to help the queen navigate the lawn in her heels. OPPOSITE: After our tour of the garden, the first lady served tea in the Yellow Oval Room to (from left) Queen Letizia's diplomatic aide, the queen, Mrs. Obama's chief of staff Tina Tchen, and me.

One of the first things on the agenda was seeking permission to plant a White House Kitchen Garden, a "learning garden" that would coordinate with her Let's Move! campaign to combat childhood obesity. Sam Kass, who served as the Obama family chef in Chicago and moved to Washington to work with them in the White House, was her staunch ally, eventually taking on the role of senior food policy advisor.

> *"The family health initiative was something that really interested the first lady; she was passionate about it. We first talked about the Kitchen Garden back in Chicago, and the idea was to plant it and, depending on how it went, we would expand it into a larger issue if it felt right. In addition to my work on the garden project, I got involved in policy, and my best day in the White House was when the school-nutrition bill was passed. The idea that 31 million kids would have fundamentally better food and that tens of millions would have access to a school breakfast — that felt pretty good. That day was euphoric."*
>
> *— Sam Kass, former Obama family chef, White House senior*
> *food policy advisor, and executive director of Let's Move!*

National Park Service permission was granted, soil was tilled, and the garden was planted in April, just three months post-inauguration. Since then, scores of schoolchildren returned year after year to plant, weed, and harvest as they learned about the food cycle and healthful eating. Not only has the 2,800-square-foot garden produced thousands of pounds of produce for the first family, for White House guests, and to aid local initiatives to feed those in need, but the Kitchen Garden was the first step in Mrs. Obama's groundbreaking work in support of child-health legislation that improved the nutrition of nearly 32 million kids who participated in school meals programs. And as the

Obamas were leaving office, the National Park Foundation received a private donation to sustain continued maintenance and preservation of the Kitchen Garden for the future.

Though I was somehow never roped into weeding or a harvest, I was always greatly inspired by the first lady's success with the Kitchen Garden, and when King Felipe VI and Queen Letizia of Spain made an official visit to Washington in September 2015, I accompanied the queen on a tour of the Kitchen Garden with Mrs. Obama while James met with the king and President Obama in the Oval Office. (I think my main role that day was one of protector, as Queen Letizia, who is petite, was wearing stiletto heels, and I was never more than a few steps away in case she took a misstep on the lawn.)

In the fall of 2013, James started living full-time in Madrid while I continued to fly between L.A., New York, Washington, and Spain, spending about ten days a month in Madrid. James served as ambassador for more than three years, and we both loved the experience of living in Spain and the energy, elegance, and grace of the people we met through his role at the embassy. We traveled extensively throughout the country, and I actually ended up opening an offshoot of my design showroom in Madrid. The U.S. embassy in Madrid is one of the few American embassies where the residence and embassy are connected. The 1950s and '60s–era buildings are sort of quirky, and the residence formerly served as a library. Like the White House, we lived above the shop: There are State Rooms on the ground floor, which we decorated in more of an American style and filled with contemporary art, and our upstairs private floor was filled with antiques and Spanish art. My idea

OPPOSITE: First Lady Michelle Obama's plane on the tarmac in Madrid in July 2016; she visited Spain on behalf of her Let Girls Learn program, which works to help educate the more than 62 million girls around the world who are not enrolled in school. RIGHT: My partner, James Costos, who served as the U.S. ambassador to Spain and Andorra from 2013 through January 2017, and I greet FLOTUS and her daughters at the Madrid airport. BELOW: James and I were at the U.S. naval base in Rota, Spain, ten days later to accompany President Obama as he delivered a speech; he stopped in Spain—it was his first official visit—following the NATO Summit in Warsaw.

LEFT: President Obama meeting with senior advisors at the embassy residence in Madrid, including (*from left*) press secretary Josh Earnest; national security advisor Susan Rice; Amy Dove, the National Security Council director for the European Union; Ambassador James Costos; and Charles Kupchan, NSC senior director for European affairs. They are seated in the upstairs living room in the residence, which I furnished with a mix of antiques and comfortable sofas and chairs. Behind the president is a panel of early 19th-century French wallpaper, which shows the Spanish occupation of Peru; I bought the antique French bookcase in Paris. POTUS stayed with James and me during this July 2016 trip; the Madrid U.S. embassy is one of the few around the world where the residence and embassy offices are located in connecting buildings. We were proud to welcome the president (and his Secret Service detail was likely pleased with the highly secure location).

was that Spaniards would primarily visit the State Floor and be immersed in American culture, and American friends would visit upstairs, and I wanted them to come away with a great appreciation for the extraordinary art and style of Spain.

In the summer of 2016, FLOTUS traveled to Morocco, Liberia, and Spain as part of her Let Girls Learn initiative on behalf of the more than 62 million young women who lack access to a school education, and we invited her and her daughters to stay with us. Not long after, the president visited Madrid on his return from a NATO conference in Warsaw; it was his first official visit to Spain, a demonstration of the country's importance as a NATO ally, and the first visit by a U.S. president in 15 years. POTUS also stayed with us, holding meetings in the embassy before we traveled together to the U.S. naval base in Rota, where he delivered a speech. The response to both of their trips to Spain was deafening—the excitement, the crowds—it was inspiring to see their influence so far from American shores. Unfortunately, President Obama was forced to shorten his trip by a day when five police officers were tragically killed in a Dallas shooting and he needed to return to the States.

I returned to Washington on Air Force One with the president, and all I can say is that the plane in the movie *Air Force One* looks exactly as it does in real life. We flew on Marine One from Joint Base Andrews, and I was excited when he asked if I wanted to stay over at the White House,

ABOVE: James and I traveled with the president on Air Force One from Madrid to Rota for his speech, though unfortunately he had to curtail his visit and return to the States because of a Dallas shooting that killed five police officers. James stayed in Spain, but I flew to Washington with POTUS and ended up staying overnight at the White House.
OPPOSITE: The president signed the flight itinerary for me in his usual teasing manner.

To Michael —
Sorry the flight wasn't up to your standards.

July 10, 2016

Our Destination: JB Andrews

Expected Arrival Time: 8:55 PM

Time Change on This Leg: Lose 6

Flight Altitude: 32,000 Feet

Average Speed: 475 MPH

We Will Fly Over: Faro, Portugal; Atlantic Ocean
& Cape May, New Jersey

Destination Weather Forecast: Partly cloudy
with Northwesterly Winds. 86 degrees.

Data connectivity and Wi-Fi available at 5Mbps
through 6 hours 15 minutes, then 10Mbps
through landing.

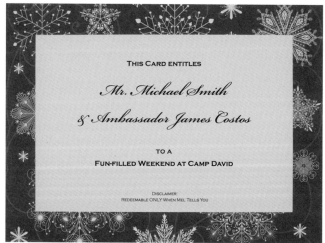

THIS CARD ENTITLES

Mr. Michael Smith

& Ambassador James Costos

TO A

FUN-FILLED WEEKEND AT CAMP DAVID

DISCLAIMER:
REDEEMABLE ONLY WHEN MEL TELLS YOU

CLOCKWISE, FROM TOP: President Obama greeting Gulf Cooperation Council leaders during a summit meeting at Camp David, the Maryland naval support facility and presidential retreat used primarily to host foreign dignitaries; near the end of the second term, the Camp David commander reached out with a request for me to refresh Aspen Lodge, the presidential cabin. In the summer of 2016, the Obamas invited James and me to join them for a weekend with a small group of their friends. An image taken by White House photographer Pete Souza at the 2012 G8 Summit shows the golf carts that are assigned to each cabin and used to navigate the property. The living room at Aspen Lodge. OPPOSITE: President and Mrs. Obama walk across the South Lawn after landing in Marine One in September 2015.

choosing the Queens' Bedroom because from a decorating standpoint it's the most original. I spent time catching up with Sasha, then took an early-morning flight the next day.

One project that I wish I had had more time and resources to focus on was Camp David, the Maryland naval support facility and presidential retreat that is used mainly to host foreign dignitaries. I was thrilled when late in the second term, the commander at Camp David asked me to refresh some of the furnishings at Aspen Lodge, the presidential cabin. Working within an almost nonexistent budget, we updated the lodge, but I had always hoped to pull in people like Ralph Lauren to make my cinematic dreams of an all-American camp come true. Sadly, time ran out. The Obamas had invited James and me to spend a weekend with them and a small group of friends that last summer, which was touching be-cause they knew that James's father had served under President Truman as a naval guard at the facility. While we were there I had a brief project meeting with FLOTUS, and after a bit she excused herself, explaining that she wanted to arrive at the dinner cabin far in advance of her guests so they would feel welcome and comfortable as soon as they walked in. It was so typical of her constant thoughtfulness and a clear reminder that punctual for Michelle Obama always means early.

10   ON HIGHER GROUND

Nearly a dozen years ago, I was asked to do some design work at Sunnylands, the fabled 200-acre former estate of Ambassador Walter Annenberg and Leonore Annenberg in Rancho Mirage, California. Decades prior, the Annenbergs had established a trust to preserve the estate as a desert retreat where world leaders could convene, and I was commissioned to do the interiors for a visitor center that architect Fred Fisher was designing on the property. As the project progressed, I became fascinated with a house that I spotted perched near the top of a mountain just across the valley. After tracking it down, I discovered that it was built in the early 1970s; once rather glamorous, it was sadly now in complete disrepair. I ended up buying it, and James and I spent a grueling few years on its restoration. It's an oasis to us.

Fast-forward to June 2013, when President Obama was staying at Sunnylands for a summit meeting with the newly elected Chinese leader, President Xi Jinping. After two long days of diplomatic sessions, the president played a few rounds of golf at the estate, and then I got a call that he would like to come over for a drink.

It was June and intensely hot, about 115 degrees, but POTUS is from Hawaii and seems to actually thrive in the heat. When he arrived, I could tell that he really liked the feeling of the house and its architecture, though his Secret Service agents seemed even more interested. We live in a double-gated community, we sit practically on top of a mountain,

OPPOSITE: Our desert house in Rancho Mirage, California, just outside Palm Springs; it is set near the top of a mountain and borders a land preserve. ABOVE: President Obama arriving at Palm Springs International Airport in February 2015.

and our property borders a land preserve. It is super convenient and unbelievably secure. High-level meetings held at Sunnylands often provided POTUS with the chance to play some golf with diplomats, staff, or friends (it's a sport that he, like many presidents, enjoys, as it's one of the few times they can be outside for any length of time), but staying at our home offered him a level of privacy hard to achieve at the retreat. One thing led to another, and before long Sunnylands was still referred to as the Western Camp David, but our week-end place became known as the unofficial Western White House.

If working on the West Coast, the first lady would also sometimes visit on her way home, and rumors were rampant in the news that the Obamas were about to buy my house or one nearby, which was definitely not the case. As their last year in office arrived, where they would settle was on everyone's mind. The president and first lady decided to stay in Washington until Sasha finished high school, and Mrs. Obama found a lovely traditional home with a garden they could rent not far from the White House. We started to work together

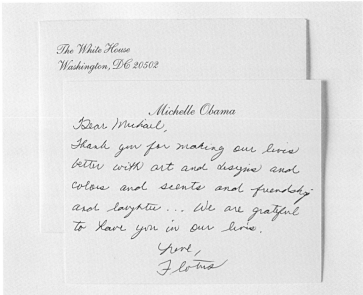

The White House
Washington, DC 20502

Michelle Obama

Dear Michael,

Thank you for making our lives better with art and design and colors and scents and friendship and laughter... We are grateful to have you in our lives.

Love,
Flotus

OPPOSITE: Malia (*left*) and Sasha Obama walk through the Cross Hall with President and Mrs. Obama and Canadian Prime Minister Justin Trudeau and his wife, Sophie Grégoire Trudeau, as they attend their first State Dinner, a March 10, 2016, event honoring the Trudeaus. CLOCKWISE, FROM TOP LEFT: I arranged for Cadogan Tate to move the Obama family's furnishings from the White House to their new residence nearby; not only are they extremely careful and patient, but they really worked with us, understanding that this would be a piecemeal process as new furniture was being regularly delivered to their warehouse and some of the White House rooms were being packed in stages. A thoughtful thank-you note from FLOTUS; I don't know how she ever found the time to write. My longtime friend Melissa Winter, Michelle Obama's deputy chief of staff, and the first lady on their way to a Hillary Clinton rally in Winston-Salem, North Carolina, on October 27, 2016, where FLOTUS gave a powerful speech in support of Secretary Clinton; Melissa now serves as chief of staff for Mrs. Obama.

STAGE & CEREMONY

Some of the country's greatest entertainers perform at the White House. National heroes are often received here. Each president and first lady symbolizes American hospitality when welcoming world leaders. Whether the occasion is a momentous bill signing, an elaborate dinner for foreign dignitaries, or the annual children's Easter Egg Roll, the White House provides a stage for moments of national celebration and ceremony.

THE STATE ROOMS

THIS PAGE: Following a two-year, $12.6 million revitalization, the National Park Service's White House Visitor Center reopened in September 2014. Located on Pennsylvania Avenue not far from the White House, the nearly 16,000-square-foot space offers a state-of-the-art experience with interactive exhibits, a museum gallery, and a retail shop. Supported by a public-private partnership, which was substantially funded by the White House Historical Association (WHHA) and bolstered by a $5 million gift from philanthropist David M. Rubenstein, the center showcases the multiple roles the White House serves—as a home, museum, office, and ceremonial stage. OPPOSITE: First Lady Michelle Obama cuts a ribbon to open the White House Visitor Center on September 10, 2014, with Fred Ryan, chairman of the WHHA, and Secretary of the Interior Sally Jewell.

on design plans, so it would be an easy transition. When I mentioned to the president and first lady that the antique tiger-maple four-poster that I loaned them for their first months in the White House was still in storage, they remembered that they loved it and ended up purchasing it for their new house. And Sasha is particularly design-oriented and had strong ideas. It was fun to work with her as if she were a regular client and we developed a sort of Sasha style for her last years at home before college.

Meanwhile, life in the White House was still going full throttle, though signs of change were becoming evident. For instance, in February we learned that the National Gallery wanted to lend an Alice Neel painting we had borrowed for the Yellow Oval Room to a European exhibition.

> *"Fortunately, most of the artworks we borrowed from museums stayed up for eight years. I remember when the National Gallery, preparing a reinstallation of the East Building in the fall of 2016, asked to have back the Susan Rothenberg painting that was hanging in the Treaty Room. This was not a return driven by the approaching end of the administration, but a work originally lent from storage being returned for public exhibition. Even so, I think that may have been the first time it hit home for the president that he would soon be leaving the White House."*
>
> **— William Allman, former White House curator**

When plans for the Canada State Dinner to be held in March started to come to fruition, the first lady realized it was time for Malia and Sasha to join their parents as they honored Prime

Minister Justin Trudeau and his wife. It was hard to believe they were grown up; they were just small children when they arrived eight years prior. Time was speeding by, and thoughts about the Obama legacy were never far from my mind—especially in terms of the White House itself.

Recognizing the impact of social media, the first lady had announced in 2015 that the 40-year ban on snapping photos on White House tours would be lifted, and there was a constant stream of new technology—amazing apps and cool 360-degree virtual tours—that brought the White House to glorious life on all digital platforms. Also, in 2014, the nearby Visitor Center had reopened following a two-year, $12.6 million revitalization. A major project largely funded by the WHHA, it includes a White House museum gallery, interactive exhibits, videos, and a retail shop that sells a range of beautiful books, presidential Christmas ornaments, and souvenirs.

"We worked on a variety of projects with First Lady Michelle Obama, including opening the Old Family Dining Room to the public tours as a showcase for contemporary art, producing the Obama White House china, the restoration of the Bellangé suite of furniture, publishing a recipe book from the Kids' State Dinners, and the opening of a revitalized White House Visitor Center.

It's a privilege for us to continue to tell the story of the improvements that a president and first lady put in place and their accomplishments while they were in office. We continue to work with them and to represent their achievements in the White House on their behalf. Certainly, their presidential libraries will do that in some measure, but we remain here, telling the story of what happened in the White House during their years as president and first lady."

—**Stewart McLaurin, president of the White House Historical Association**

OPPOSITE: As per presidential tradition, President Obama invited President-Elect Donald Trump for a meeting in the Oval Office on November 10, 2016, two days following the election. CLOCKWISE, FROM RIGHT: President Obama leaves the East Room on January 17, 2017, after taking a group photo with the General Services Administration (GSA) staff. President Obama walks to the West Colonnade after leaving the Oval Office for the last time on January 20, 2017. I was surprised and amused that L.A.–based artist Kimberly Brooks decided to honor my work with hers at the January 21, 2017, Women's March on Washington.

CLOCKWISE, FROM TOP LEFT: James and I stand steps away from President and Mrs. Obama in a Joint Base Andrews hangar on January 20, 2017, as the former president speaks to staff, friends, military members, and supporters who gathered to say goodbye before the Obamas' flight departed for California; his address was a heartfelt and poignant thank-you to everyone in the room, many of whom had worked with them throughout their two terms. James and I were already seated on the Presidential Aircraft as we watched the Obamas approach the stairs to the plane. President and Mrs. Obama were honored by a military cordon as they walked down the crimson carpet during the departure ceremony. OPPOSITE: The Obama family came to stay with us in Rancho Mirage for a few days to decompress.

And in truth, everyone was assuming there would be an easy, seamless transfer of power to the next administration. The Clintons had lived in the Residence for eight years, and Secretary Clinton was a familiar presence during her service as Secretary of State. Residence staff are nonpartisan, often working through the course of several presidential transitions, but I had the sense that many were anticipating a happy homecoming. In addition, after many collaborative projects, a strong, genuine friendship had developed among the Bushes, the Clintons, and the Obamas. There was a clear expectation of goodwill, one that never came to pass.

Though it wasn't announced until early February 2017, after a raft of rumors the president-elect and Mrs. Trump chose to work with a New York–based designer named Tham Kannalikham on their interiors. We didn't meet until after the inauguration, but Tham reached out in December and we had some friendly calls and emails as I did my best to explain the complex logistics involved with the Inauguration Day move-in, as well as the project in general. The Bushes had been impeccable during our transition, and the Obamas wanted to exceed the high bar they had set. In the meantime, as I was finalizing the Obamas' move to their new house, James and I learned that we would have to vacate the Madrid embassy by the morning of the inauguration, far earlier than expected. (During presidential transitions, ambassadors must submit resignations the December after an election, but extensions are the norm, allowing for diplomatic continuity on foreign soil.)

We swiftly found a beautiful flat in Madrid, as we were enjoying our life in Spain. After do-

nating much of our embassy decor to the State Department, we moved into our new place, shipped remaining furnishings back to the States, and headed to Washington as our incredible friends and staff in Madrid helped oversee the rushed conclusion to James's commission.

The Obamas had taken their annual Christmas holiday in Hawaii but planned to take another brief trip following the inauguration to decompress before they settled in their new home. Everyone decided it made sense for them to spend a few days with us in the desert. Over the past few years, I had worked to make the Obamas' visits to our house as easy as possible—including air-conditioning the garages that were used as the Secret Service outpost and making sure their security detail was comfortable and well-fed. They are an extraordinary team. Under the special circumstances, James and I wanted this family visit to be flawless.

Pre-inauguration, I was asked to appear on ABC News with the late Cokie Roberts to describe the logistics of a White House move-in, and it was surreal to be on the other side of that transition, in a scenario so drastically different from that of 2008. On Inauguration Day, James and I headed to Joint Base Andrews, where we watched the ceremony in a room with a small group of friends. Not long after, the Obamas arrived to speak to a gathering of a few hundred staff, military personnel, friends, and supporters in a large hangar before leaving for Palm Springs. I imagine this traditional goodbye is unbelievably emotional for all outgoing leaders and their teams; I know the experience will remain seared in my own

OPPOSITE: President Obama speaks at the National Portrait Gallery on February 12, 2018, where his portrait, by Kehinde Wiley, and that of Mrs. Obama, by Amy Sherald, were unveiled to the public. ABOVE: The Obamas with their portraits and the artists, Kehinde Wiley (*left*) and Amy Sherald. RIGHT: The president's portrait hangs in the museum's America's Presidents gallery, and Mrs. Obama's portrait proved to be so popular, it was moved from its original location to a more spacious gallery. The paintings were commissioned by the National Portrait Gallery and paid for by private funding; part of the museum's permanent collection, next year they are scheduled to embark on a yearlong exhibition tour at museums in Chicago, Brooklyn, L.A., Atlanta, and Houston.

LEFT: On November 13, 2018, Michelle Obama kicked off the book tour for her hugely successful memoir, *Becoming*, at Chicago's Seminary Co-op bookstore; the autobiography immediately broke sales records, selling millions of copies worldwide, and was recently adapted and released as a Netflix documentary. BELOW: Former senior advisor to the Obama White House and longtime friend and colleague Valerie Jarrett interviews Mrs. Obama at the Capital One Arena in Washington, D.C., part of her sold-out, multicity, international tour of talks and book signings; Valerie is now senior advisor to the Obama Foundation.

memory. President Obama's remarks that day were so poignant; his words were heartfelt as he thanked everyone for their extraordinary support over the past eight years. It was deeply emotional, as eight years seemed like a lifetime to everyone there.

Someone on George W. Bush's team had thoughtfully suggested that a small group of friends and longtime staff should fly to California with the Obama family before heading back to Washington on the plane's return flight; a handful joined us as we departed for California on the Presidential Aircraft, previously designated as Air Force One. Near the end of the flight, we hit massive turbulence from a winter storm, and after two aborted landings we had to be diverted to an air base about an hour away. We joined the motorcade to Rancho Mirage, and the Obamas' new life began with a relaxing dinner for family and friends in front of a warm fire.

Following a brief respite, we all got back to work. I had been particularly fascinated with one project that had started a few years earlier, when I was asked to consult on the selection of artists being considered for the two sets of official portraits that are produced for each presidential administration. One set of portraits of the president and first lady are commissioned and funded by the National Portrait Gallery for its permanent collection, and a second set of paintings to be displayed in the White House is paid for by the WHHA. Bill Allman was also advising, but my friend Thelma Golden was spearheading the project, as she is a longtime ally of the Obamas and a true force in the American art world. Her career has soared after her incredibly well-regarded turn as curator at the Whitney, and now as director and chief curator of the extraordinary Studio Museum in Harlem.

There was an enormous, very wide range of talents to consider, and the president and first lady took a great deal of interest in the various artists, meeting a few of them with Thelma. The president was particularly intrigued by the creative process and the intellectual aspects of the project. We compiled a shortlist for consideration, and they carefully made their decisions. For the National Portrait Gallery, Kehinde Wiley was selected to paint the president, and Amy Sherald was chosen for Mrs. Obama; both were brilliant choices. (The artists for the White House portraits were chosen simultaneously but will be announced at a later date.)

I learned so much about portraiture through this process—which is ironic, as I often describe my interior design work as creating a portrait of a person. It was amazing to watch these static canvases absolutely spring to life in the hands of Kehinde and Amy. I find the paintings to be powerful and heroic, but I don't think any of us anticipated the mind-blowing response they received when they were revealed at the National Portrait Gallery in February 2018. By March 2020, more than four million visitors had flocked to the museum to view the portraits, which will embark on an extended five-city national tour in 2021. Though reaction by art critics was positive and negative, the popular response to the works was unprecedented; both monumental and highly charged, it was but one reflection of the powerful continued relevance of Barack and Michelle Obama in the world at large.

Having served as a young presidential family, the Obamas now have the opportunity to connect and empower from a nonpartisan platform, one removed from political divisiveness. The global community strongly identifies with them—from the blockbuster success of Mrs. Obama's memoir, *Becoming*, to the constant fascination with the couple's seasonal playlists and reading recommendations to the rapt attention paid to their social media posts. They are inspiring yet approachable, both authoritative and authentic.

> *"I think civic engagement as a mechanism for improving our world has always been at the essence of the Obamas' work. Beginning with his days as a community organizer and her days working in the mayor's office in Chicago – it's all about being of service, being a powerful force for good. The heartbeat of the White House was those Americans whose lives were going to be impacted by our policy decisions. We spent time and energy thinking about how to give them the sense that their opinions, views, and perspectives were valued, how to help people feel comfortable, that they belonged. People are at their best when they feel that they belong. I think that the relationships that rippled out across the world during their eight years in office are just the foundation of the relationships that will develop through the Obama Presidential Center.*
>
> *The Center will be an incredible beacon of hope on the South Side of Chicago, but its reach will extend to every corner of the world because of civic engagement, because of the Obamas' ability to reach out to connect and convene. They give people a sense of empowerment, an empowerment that then enables those people to go back out into the world to do good work.*
>
> *The Obamas' legacy will include the literally millions of people they empowered – especially Americans, making them feel that the White House belonged to them and that their thoughts, their dreams, and their aspirations truly mattered. President Obama always wants to give people the tools to do their best and help others. That work will continue for the rest of their lives through the Obama Foundation. I see it as a seamless arc between their presidency and their future. The foundation is the platform by which they'll be able to continue that work."*
>
> *—Valerie Jarrett, former senior advisor to President Barack Obama*

Before the president and first lady left office, plans for their Obama Foundation were well underway, and I was asked to help convene a small group of design experts to recommend potential architects for the future Obama Presidential Center. POTUS felt strongly that it

shouldn't be a traditional museum, but more of a community center, a place that was very much active, alive, and energizing. It was essential to document his remarkable social and political path as well as his historic presidency, but not in a conventional manner. He also wanted to locate the center in Chicago, his wife's hometown and the place that launched his life of public service. He envisioned a center that would reenergize the city's South Side and engage others to become more involved in their communities.

After careful deliberation, the Obama Foundation selected New York architects Tod Wil-

liams and Billie Tsien of TWBTA to design the Obama Presidential Center, which will be located in Chicago's Jackson Park and comprise four buildings, including a 235-foot-tall museum structure. The campus is conceived to be a public gathering place, including a forum with training rooms and an auditorium, an athletic facility, a branch of the Chicago Public Library, and a park and playground for neighbors and visitors to enjoy.

But the OPC represents far more than its buildings: It will reflect the Obamas' continuing mission to "inspire, empower, and connect people to change their world." The initiatives the president and first lady supported in the White House have since expanded, with goals of training the next generation of leaders, empowering adolescent girls around the world through education, ensuring boys and young men of color can reach their full potential, and creating pathways to opportunity for those who have been traditionally underserved always top of mind. I feel so privileged to have worked with them for more than a decade. The endless possibilities for their continuing impact on our country and the world are astounding—and I am thrilled to watch them unfold.

ABOVE: President and Mrs. Obama take the stage in Chicago at the first Obama Foundation Summit on October 31, 2017. OPPOSITE: A rendering of the Obama Presidential Center campus, which was designed by architects Tod Williams and Billie Tsien of TWBTA and will be built in Jackson Park on the South Side of Chicago.

ACKNOWLEDGMENTS

I'd like to acknowledge so many of the people who helped me — both in bringing this book to fruition and also those who worked with me throughout the eight years that I was involved in the White House project. First, I'd like to thank Margaret Russell, who supported my work on the presidential project from its inception and then helped me bring this book to life with her keen eye and editorial insight. I would also like to thank the Rizzoli team, especially Charles Miers and Kathleen Jayes, for producing such a beautiful crystallization of this important moment in history.

Thank you to Sam Shahid, who always lends his timeless sense of clarity and balance to each and every page, and to photographer Michael Mundy, who captures beauty and nuance in every image. I appreciate the care and attention that Matthew Kraus, Leigh Montville, and Carolyn Burbridge gave to the project, and the kind assistance of photographers Roger Davies, Lawrence Jackson, Chuck Kennedy, and Amanda Lucidon, as well as the support of Steven Booth, Susan Bartlett Crater, and Caitlin Sanders, who provided access to needed film. A special thank-you to Pete Souza, President Obama's chief official White House photographer, who has been a powerful voice in sustaining the digital legacy of the Obama administration.

I would like to thank everyone who took the time to discuss our shared experiences, especially Molly Donovan, Ferial Govashiri, Valerie Jarrett, Sam Kass, Alyssa Mastromonaco, Stewart McLaurin, Andrew Pickard Morgan, Angella Reid, Shonda Rhimes, Desirée Rogers, and George Stephanopoulos. Melissa Winter, a dear friend, deserves special thanks for her loyal support since our very first design review at the Hay-Adams hotel.

My team in Los Angeles, who worked tirelessly on this design project, should take great pride in what we accomplished together; thank you for your amazing work. Special kudos to Camilla Hansen, Mark Matuszak, Michele Miyakoda, and Marc Szafran.

There were a few particularly challenging projects over the years, and I will never forget the commitment and dedication of Bob Clark, Bob Truax, Nicholas Fox Weber, and Adam Weinberg; you made miracles happen. I am also deeply grateful to all the people who made our creative work in the White House possible—especially the museum curators who lent us the wonderful paintings that brought a new energy to the Residence. To the dozens of artisans, vendors, and workers who helped me make this White House not just a home for a remarkable young family, but a testament to a particular moment in American history, I thank you from the bottom of my heart.

I'd like to thank the White House staff in the Residence and the East and West Wings, who were unfailingly patient and gracious; from butlers to florists to electricians, you often made the impossible come true. I will be forever indebted to William "Bill" Allman, who is not only a legendary curator and a brilliant historian, but also a dear friend. From looking out for me on my very first day at the White House to reviewing every page of this book, he has been an unwavering support.

My greatest appreciation goes to the Obama family—the president, first lady, Malia, Sasha, and Mrs. Robinson. Thank you for including me on this incredible and sometimes wild ride through time and history. You are a constant inspiration. Your public service and devotion to the American people set an exceptional example that we must always strive to be the best that we can be, and to be known by our actions as well as our words.

And most important, I'd like to thank my partner, James, for always being so supportive and such a great sounding board in everything and in life.

—Michael S. Smith

PHOTOGRAPHY CREDITS

Page 6: Miller Mobley/August. **Page 10:** Michael Mundy. **Page 12:** Gary Hershorn/REUTERS. **Page 14,** clockwise from top: Björn Wallander; *Houses* cover, Grey Crawford, photo by Roger Davies; *Elements of Style* cover, Michael Mundy. **Page 16,** from top: Pete Souza, courtesy Barack Obama Presidential Library; Jae C. Hong/AP Photo. **Page 17,** from left: Charles Ommanney/Getty Images; Callie Shell. **Page 18:** Roger Davies. **Pages 20-21:** Frank Franklin II/AP Photo; Joe Raedle/Getty Images News. **Page 23:** Oli Scarff/Getty Images News. **Page 24:** Library of Congress, Geography and Maps Division. **Page 27:** Buyenlarge via Getty. **Pages 28-29:** ©2000 White House Historical Association (WHHA); ©1962 WHHA, courtesy Historical Society of Pennsylvania. **Page 30:** Benjamin Henry Latrobe, Library of Congress. **Page 31,** from top: Anonymous, WHHA; Samuel Blodget, Jr., White House Collection/WHHA. **Page 32,** clockwise from top left: Benjamin Henry Latrobe, courtesy Maryland Historical Society; Erik Kvalsvik, White House Collection/WHHA; William Strickland, Library of Congress. **Page 33:** Erik Kvalsvik, ©2004 WHHA. **Page 35,** clockwise from top left: ©1966 WHHA; ©2001 WHHA; ©2000 WHHA; ©2000 WHHA. **Page 36,** clockwise from top left: White House Collection/WHHA; ©2000 WHHA; ©1962 WHHA; ©2000 WHHA. **Page 37,** clockwise from top left: ©WHHA; ©2000 WHHA; ©1962 WHHA. **Page 38,** clockwise from top left: ©WHHA; ©2000 WHHA; ©2000 WHHA; White House Collection/WHHA; ©1999 WHHA. **Page 39:** ©2000 WHHA. **Page 40,** clockwise from top left: White House Collection/WHHA; ©2000 WHHA; ©1962 WHHA; ©2000 WHHA; ©2000 WHHA. **Page 41,** clockwise from top left: ©2000 WHHA; ©2000 WHHA; ©2019 Andrew Wyeth/Artists Rights Society (ARS), New York. **Pages 42-43,** from left: White House Collection/WHHA; ©2007 Peter Waddell for the WHHA. **Page 44:** White House Collection. **Page 46,** from top: White House Collection; National Archives and Records Administration. **Page 47,** clockwise from top left: National Archives and Records Administration; ©2006 Peter Waddell for the WHHA; Frances Benjamin Johnston, Library of Congress. **Pages 48, 50-51:** ©1904 Detroit Photographic Company, Library of Congress. **Page 52,** from top: Lorenzo Winslow Papers, White House Collection; Frances Benjamin Johnston, Library of Congress. **Page 53,** from top: White House Collection; Library of Congress. **Pages 54-55:** Abbie Rowe, National Park Service; Everett Collection Inc./Alamy Stock Photo. **Pages 56-58:** Abbie Rowe, National Park Service. **Page 59,** clockwise from top left: Abbie Rowe, National Park Service (2); United States Navy, Harry S. Truman Library & Museum. **Page 60:** CBS Photo Archive/Getty Images. **Pages 62-63:** Ed Clark/The LIFE Picture Collection/Getty Images; Mark Shaw ©1961 Time Inc., photo by Roger Davies. **Pages 64-65:** Courtesy Susan Bartlett Crater/Sister Parish Design; courtesy John F. Kennedy Presidential Library and Museum, Boston. **Pages 66-67:** Robert Knudsen, courtesy JFK Library. **Pages 68-69:** George F. Mobley ©1963 WHHA. **Page 70:** Cecil Stoughton, courtesy JFK Library. **Pages 73-77:** Robert Knudsen, courtesy JFK Library. **Page 78:** Robert Knudsen, courtesy LBJ Library. **Page 79,** from top: Frank Wolfe, courtesy LBJ Library; Mike Geissinger, courtesy LBJ Library. **Page 80,** from top: Richard Nixon Presidential Library and Museum/NARA; courtesy Gerald R. Ford Presidential Library & Museum. **Page 81,** from top: David Hume Kennerly, courtesy Gerald R. Ford Presidential Library; ©1974 WHHA. **Page 82,** from top: Derry Moore/*Architectural Digest*, ©CondéNast; Mary Anne Fackelman, courtesy Ronald Reagan Presidential Library and Museum/NARA. **Page 83,** from top: Derry Moore/*Architectural Digest*, ©Condé Nast; George H.W. Bush Presidential Library and Museum. **Page 84,** from top: Bruce White ©2000 WHHA; Bruce White ©1999 WHHA. **Page 85:** Peter Vitale ©2003 WHHA; Peter Vitale ©WHHA. **Page 86,** from top: Bruce White ©2000 WHHA; Erik Kvalsvik ©2005 WHHA. **Page 87:** Bruce White ©2000 WHHA. **Pages 88-89:** Ron Edmonds/AP Photo; David Hume Kennerly/Getty Images News. **Page 91,** from top: Courtesy whitehousemuseum.org (2); Roger Davies. **Page 92:** Joyce N. Boghosian, Official White House photos, courtesy George W. Bush Presidential Library and Museum. **Page 93,** from top: Joyce N. Boghosian, Official White House photo, courtesy George W. Bush Presidential Library and Museum; courtesy of Michael S Smith Inc.; Joyce N. Boghosian, Official White House photo, courtesy George W. Bush Presidential Library and Museum. **Page 95:** Courtesy Michael S Smith Inc. **Page 96,** from top: Peter Foley/EPA/Shutterstock; Paul Morse. **Page 97:** Win McNamee/Getty Images. **Pages 98-103:** Courtesy Michael S Smith Inc. **Page 104:** Charles Ommanney/Getty Images. **Pages 106-7:** Annie Leibovitz/Trunk Archive; Glyn Lowe Photoworks. **Pages 108-9:** Jim West/Alamy Stock Photo; Roger Davies. **Page 111,** from top: David Hume Kennerly/Getty Images News; Pete Souza, courtesy Barack Obama Library. **Page 112,** from top: Pete Souza, American Photo Archive/Alamy Stock Photo; Pete Souza, courtesy Barack Obama Library. **Page 113:** Joe Fox Berlin, Radharc Images/Alamy Stock Photo. **Page 115,** clockwise from top: Pete Souza, White House Photo/Alamy Stock Photo; Mark Matuszak, courtesy Michael S Smith Inc.; courtesy Michael S Smith Inc. **Pages 116-17:** Doug Mills/*The New York Times*/Redux ©*The New York Times*; Matthew D'Agostino ©2015 WHHA. **Page 119,** from top: Courtesy Michael S Smith; courtesy Barack Obama Library. **Page 120:** Lawrence Jackson, courtesy Barack Obama Library. **Page 123:** Noah Tucker Design, courtesy Michael S Smith Inc.; Lawrence Jackson, courtesy Barack Obama Library. **Page 124:** Michael Mundy. **Pages 126-27:** Roger Davies; Mark Matuszak, courtesy Michael S Smith Inc. **Pages 128-32:** Michael Mundy. **Page 133:** Mark Matuszak, courtesy Michael S Smith Inc. **Pages 134-36:** Michael Mundy. **Pages 138-39:** Courtesy Michael S Smith Inc. **Page 140:** Roger Davies. **Page 141,** clockwise from top left: Courtesy Michael S Smith Inc.; Roger Davies; courtesy Baker Furniture; courtesy Michael S Smith Inc. (2); courtesy Elizabeth Dow (2); courtesy Michael S Smith Inc. **Pages 142-44:** Michael Mundy. **Pages 146-47:** Roger Davies; Mark Matuszak, courtesy Michael S Smith Inc. **Pages 148-49:** Michael Mundy; Chuck Kennedy, courtesy Barack Obama Library. **Pages 150-57:** Michael Mundy. **Pages 158-59:** Roger

First published in the United States of America in 2020 by
Rizzoli International Publications, Inc.
300 Park Avenue South
New York, NY 10010
www.rizzoliusa.com

Copyright © 2020 Michael S. Smith
Text by Margaret Russell
Foreword by Michelle Obama

Quote on page 267: Courtesy Barack Obama Presidential Library
The publisher gratefully acknowledges the considerable assistance and many photographs
provided by the Barack Obama Presidential Library and the White House Historical Association (WHHA), without which this book would not be possible.

Design by Sam Shahid
Art Direction by Matthew Kraus

Publisher: Charles Miers
Senior Editor: Kathleen Jayes
Production Manager: Colin Hough-Trapp
Color production: Carolyn Burbridge
Photo research: Margaret Russell
Photo permissions: Leigh Montville
Managing Editor: Lynn Scrabis

Printed in Italy

2020 2021 2022 2023 / 10 9 8 7 6 5 4 3 2

ISBN: 978-0-8478-6479-9
Library of Congress Control Number: 2020937208

Visit us online:
Facebook.com/RizzoliNewYork
Twitter: @Rizzoli_Books
Instagram.com/RizzoliBooks
Pinterest.com/RizzoliBooks
Youtube.com/user/RizzoliNY
Issuu.com/Rizzoli